BILLIE EILISH IS LIFE

A Superfan's Guide to
All Things We Love about Billie Eilish

KATHLEEN PERRICONE
ILLUSTRATED BY CAROLINA FUENMAYOR

CONTENTS

Introduction 5

Part One: Billie the G.O.A.T. 9

Musical Prodigy 11

    Sweet Sixteen 19

    Best New Artist 27

    Pursuit of Happiness 35

    Girl, Interrupted 41

Part Two: Stream Queen 49

    Discography 51

Part Three: Billie Bossa Nova 75

    Billie A to Z 77

Part Four: What She Was Made For . . . 111

    Reinvented Pop Star 113

    Sibling Synergy 125

    Hard, Yet Soft 131

    Young and Restless 137

    Birds of a Feather 149

Acknowledgments 159

About the Author 159

INTRODUCTION

One of the most remarkable young talents in music today, Billie Eilish Pirate Baird O'Connell—yes, that's her real name!—is in a class all her own. She writes and produces her own songs (with her brother and longtime collaborator, Finneas), directs her music videos, and completely controls every aspect of her image. This specific brand of pop star prefers baggy clothes, sings about monsters and misogyny, and advocates for mental health, all while racking up billions of streams of her Grammy-winning catalog. And she's been doing it since the tender age of thirteen, when her song "ocean eyes" became a viral sensation on SoundCloud in 2015. "Everything could be easier if I wanted it to, but I'm not that kind of person and I'm not that kind of artist," Billie revealed to *The New York Times*, just as her career began to take off. "I'd rather die than be that kind of artist."

In 2019, Billie's breakout No. 1 hit, "bad guy," officially introduced the world to an enchanting enigma: a green-haired, Gucci-wearing teenager who referred to everyone as "dude" and was obsessed with Justin Bieber (now one of her closest friends). In the few years since, she's grown up before our very eyes, especially as an artist.

> *"She's creating her diary . . . vocally," praised Rihanna.*

With the record-breaking success of her debut album, *WHEN WE ALL FALL ASLEEP, WHERE DO WE GO?*, the seventeen-year-old earned the distinction of being the youngest artist ever to be nominated in the Grammy Awards' Big Four general categories—Album of the Year, Record of the Year, Song of the Year, and Best New Artist—and only the second person in history to win all four. In 2020, Billie also became the youngest artist to record a James Bond theme song, for *No Time to Die*, Daniel Craig's final portrayal of the iconic spy. It turned out to be a blockbuster for Billie, who won the Academy Award for Best Original Song in 2022. Unbelievably, just two years later, at the age of twenty-two, she made Hollywood history with her second song written for a film, *Barbie*'s "What Was I Made For?," setting the record for youngest person to win two Oscars in any category.

Billie is undeniably the voice of Generation Z—though seemingly everyone is listening. On Spotify alone, she has more than 100 million monthly listeners. Her 2024 album, *HIT ME HARD AND SOFT*, surpassed 500 million streams in its first week alone. Another 120 million fans follow the superstar on Instagram. With such great power, of course, comes great responsibility, and Billie uses her global platform to raise awareness about the issues nearest to her heart, like women's rights, LGBTQ+ rights, animal rights, body positivity, climate change, and sustainability for future generations.

In the process, she has earned the respect of pop icons who paved her way, most notably the best-selling female recording artist of the twenty-first century: Rihanna. In a 2024 interview with *Access Hollywood*, the Fenty Beauty mogul described Billie as "the coolest girl ever" and her dream musical collaboration. "She's creating her diary . . . vocally," praised Rihanna. "You can feel that she's zoned into who she is and what she's experienced, and what she's feeling, even if she doesn't know what it is."

PART ONE

Billie the G.O.A.T.

MUSICAL PRODIGY

Anything that Billie Eilish dreamed of doing as a kid could be explored within the walls of her family's two-bedroom bungalow in Highland Park, a middle-class suburb of Los Angeles. If she wanted to play music, there were four guitars, three pianos, and a ukulele at her disposal. When she became interested in photography, she borrowed her father's digital camera and staged shoots with her toys in the backyard. At the age of six, her parents decided to homeschool Billie and her older brother, Finneas, following an informal curriculum that prioritized their individual artistic interests.

Billie's favorite subjects were songwriting (taught by her mother, Maggie Baird, an actress who made appearances on *Friends* and *The X-Files*), as well as singing and dancing, which she studied at the Los Angeles Children's Chorus and Revolution Dance Studio, respectively. Her father, Patrick O'Connell, an actor-turned-carpenter, shaped the children's music tastes with mixtapes of artists like Avril Lavigne, Linkin Park, Sarah McLachlan, and the Beatles. In 2008, seven-year-old Billie chose the British band's 1968 song "Happiness Is a Warm Gun" to perform at her second talent show (her first performance had been "Tomorrow" from the musical *Annie*). It was around that time she picked up the ukulele and, with the three chords she knew, wrote her first song: "What a Wonderful Life," she recalled a decade later in 2019 as she strummed the tiny four-string guitar to serenade James Corden during "Carpool Karaoke," a popular segment on his former CBS program, *The Late Late Show*.

When Billie was twelve, she recorded her first track, "Fingers Crossed," about a zombie apocalypse, for her mother's songwriting class. "The little assignment was that you had to watch a movie or a TV show and then write down all the parts that you thought were good hooks or good lyrics," she explained to Junkee. "So, I watched *The Walking Dead*—like, why not—and then I wrote down all this stuff . . . it sounds more like a longing heartbreak song, but nope, it's about zombies."

Despite her musical talent, dancing remained Billie's passion, and she spent twelve hours a week practicing tap, ballet, hip-hop, and contemporary at Revolution. No one knew she was also a gifted singer until the school's annual sleepover, when students are encouraged to perform something they're good at other than dance. Billie decided to sing "Secret"

HORSE GIRL

Ever since she was a kid, Billie has had a deep connection with horses, "one of the only things that bring me peace," she told Dutch radio's 3voor12 in 2019. "I love them, they're such beautiful creatures." However, horseback riding lessons can be pricey—and Billie's parents simply couldn't afford them. So, in exchange for lessons, she worked for two years at a local horse camp, cleaning the stables and bridling the animals for other equestrians. It was exhausting for the young girl, both physically and mentally. "I made a couple of friends, but otherwise nobody was very nice," Billie revealed to *Rolling Stone*. "Horse people don't like poor people." Years later, after her debut album hit No. 1 on the charts, the singer had plenty of her own money to invest in her childhood hobby. In 2019, Billie returned to the stable where she was once shunned to lease her own horse, which cost $1,000 a month. While there, she stopped by the barn and reunited with a black mare named Jackie O. "I was literally in love with this horse," Billie gushed to *Rolling Stone*. "Even after I stopped riding, I came here just to be with her."

by Australian singer-songwriter Missy Higgins. "It was the first time I'd ever performed for a group of people that I knew really, besides talent shows and stuff on my own," she recalled in her 2021 photography book *Billie Eilish*. "I looked up to all these girls. I thought they were all cool. I was so nervous. My voice was all shaky. My voice cracked like five times. I was terrible. And I remember thinking, 'Oh God, they're gonna think I suck.'"

They didn't—in fact everyone told Billie she was so great that maybe one day she could share the stage with another Revolution alum: R&B singer Tinashe, whose debut single "2 On" was one of the biggest hits of 2014. "I was like, 'Never. I would never,'" Billie recalled in her photo book.

Billie's dance instructor, Fred Diaz, was so impressed that in the fall of 2015, he asked the thirteen-year-old to record an original song that he would choreograph for their next recital. Instead of submitting her zombie ode, she went with "ocean eyes," a sleepy dream-pop track that her seventeen-year-old brother, Finneas, had written for his band. "I loved it and I couldn't get it out of my head for weeks," she recalled to *Vogue*. Billie and Finneas recorded the song on his iMac, but before she got the chance to perform to it at her recital, she injured the growth plate in her hip during practice. The injury ended her dancing dreams but jumpstarted her musical ambitions. In November, the siblings uploaded "ocean eyes" to SoundCloud, a streaming platform where they had previously posted two other songs "for fun and for our friends to listen to," she told *Vogue*. But "ocean eyes" was different. By the next morning, it had a thousand plays. "I would hit refresh and it would have a bunch of new plays," Billie said. "We were like, 'What the hell is going on?'"

> *"I remember thinking, 'Oh God, they're gonna think I suck.'"*

Finneas, who had dabbled in acting like his parents and made appearances on *Glee* and *Modern Family*, already had a manager, Danny Rukasin. Rukasin came over to the Baird-O'Connell home that day for a family meeting about what the teens should do to capitalize on the momentum. "We discussed whether or not this was something Billie was really interested in doing or just a hobby," Rukasin recalled to Music Business Worldwide. "It was still early stages, but she had a vision of how she wanted what she was doing to be put out in the world."

In January 2016, Rukasin arranged a deal with Platoon, a London-based artist development company that specialized in fine-tuning emerging artists. He also hired a publicist and stylist for the fourteen-year-old, as "ocean eyes" racked up two million plays on

SoundCloud. The song reached the ears of Zane Lowe, a DJ for Apple Music's brand-new 24/7 radio station, who buzzed about the "absolutely incredible" young talent. "Meet Billie Eilish, Pop's Next It Girl," declared *Vogue* that August.

In her interview with the fashion magazine, the teen—who was still healing from her dance injury—opened up about how she and Finneas were motivated to take the leap from playing music in his bedroom. Not only were they writing more songs, but they were also doing "little shows here and there just to get used to the idea of performing in front of people. I mean, I've always been a performer because of dance and going to competitions and being in the children's chorus. I even used to do plays when I was little. I know how to be in front of an audience, so I'm not terrified."

PIRATE, THE POP STAR?

If you thought the name Billie Eilish was peculiar, that's only the half of it. The singer's parents, Maggie Baird and Patrick O'Connell, originally intended to name their daughter Eilish after watching a documentary on conjoined twins Katie and Eilish Holton, who were surgically separated in 1992 (unfortunately, Katie didn't survive the procedure). Older brother Finneas, who was four at the time, suggested Pirate for his unborn sister, and the name stuck for several months, until Maggie and Patrick ultimately decided to honor her late father, Bill, who passed away in February 2001, by calling their baby girl Billie—making her official (and very long) name Billie Eilish Pirate Baird O'Connell. Growing up, she went by Billie O'Connell, although she never liked it, the seventeen-year-old confessed to *Rolling Stone* in 2019: "It sounds like if a goat was a person: Billie Goat O'Connell." She didn't want to evoke a swashbuckling pirate either, so she adopted only one of her two middle names to become the pop star we all know and love: Billie Eilish.

SWEET SIXTEEN

One of the millions of music fans who discovered "ocean eyes" on SoundCloud was an Interscope Records intern, who passed on the link to executives, including Justin Lubliner. The twenty-five-year-old wunderkind had just launched his own label, Darkroom, and he desperately wanted Billie, who he dubbed "a new breed of pop star," on his roster. "Within one second of hearing it and seeing her photo, it just clicked—my radar went off," Lubliner recalled to *HITS*. "I felt like this was the artist that I'd been searching for my entire career. I was going to make sure I did everything possible to work with her."

Billie, who was still only fourteen, met with Lubliner, one of the countless music execs courting the punky pop phenom. But this time felt different. "He was the only person out of everyone I met that year—and I met with a lot of people—that really saw something and believed it," she told *Billboard*. "He didn't have some plan that was to turn me into something different. He really just saw me for exactly who I was and wanted to support that. I think that's rare." In August 2016, four months shy of Billie's fifteenth birthday, she and Finneas signed with Darkroom, a record label under Interscope, and immediately got to work on their first release, an eight-song extended play (EP) she titled *dont smile at me*, which they recorded in Finneas's makeshift studio in his bedroom.

Despite the siblings' relative inexperience—Finneas was only nineteen himself—Lubliner and his team stepped back and gave them full autonomy, "which is insane, because some labels really control everything you do," Billie told Junkee. "I always know what I want to do. So with that, I didn't even talk to anybody, I didn't ask anybody, I was like, 'Okay, this is the order of the songs, these are all the songs that are gonna be on the EP, I want the EP cover to be me in red on a red ladder, in a yellow room, with a bunch of chains on. And the EP is called *dont smile at me*. That's it. Boom. Bye.' And then they were like, 'Okay.'"

Darkroom also listened to Billie's suggestion to put out several singles in the months ramping up to the EP's August 2017 release, beginning with her viral sensation "ocean eyes." She next introduced the duality of her artistry with "bellyache," written from the perspective of a psychotic killer, which charted in more than a dozen countries, from the US and UK to Slovakia. In case there was any question, the teen assured everyone the song was not personal. "It's really fun to put yourself into a character—into

THE GIFT OF TIME

For Billie, being successful at such a young age was a double-edged sword. While promoting her debut EP, *dont smile at me*, the singer was repeatedly asked the same question: "What's it like being fifteen?" "Oh my God, I don't know," she vented to *Harper's Bazaar* in 2017. "I've never been older." The following year brought a different perspective. "When people are like, 'Oh my God, you're so young,' it's like, 'well, not to me,'" the sixteen-year-old explained to *Complex*'s Pigeons and Planes. "There's a lot of advantages to being young, especially in this kind of place I'm in, I guess. If you do something when you're really young, that's impressive." With age, Billie gained even more insight. Although she admittedly missed out on being a "normal" teenager, she was grateful to have been discovered at thirteen. "If it happened later, then people would be able to dig up dirt from when I was that age," Billie joked during a 2019 appearance on *The Howard Stern Show* when she was seventeen. "Like, if this hadn't happened at that age, I would have been doing some reckless shit."

> *"Billie Eilish breaks boundaries in all that she does. She is amongst the most influential musicians of her generation... The future is bright for Billie."*

shoes you wouldn't normally be in," she explained to *Billboard*. "You don't have to be in love with someone to write a song about being in love with someone. You don't have to hate somebody to write a song about hating somebody. You don't have to kill people to write a song about killing people. I'm not going to kill people, so I'm just going to become another character."

Five singles later, by the time *dont smile at me* dropped, Billie already had a quarter-million followers on Instagram, had sold out concerts, and got recognized by fans on the street. A search of her name on Google yielded 1.13 million results. Apple Music also helped boost her visibility by naming Billie its Up Next Artist, a coveted title that included an interview on the platform's popular Apple Music 1 (previously Beats 1) radio show; her own documentary, called *The World's a Little Blurry*; and a music debut on CBS's *The Late Late Show with James Corden*. "Billie is an amazing modern pop star," praised Apple's Zane Lowe. "For someone so young, she's got such a clear vision about the way she wants her music to be delivered and presented. We're already getting a really diverse collection of sounds from her. Billie can hit three or four different styles over three or four different songs, and it's exciting as a music fan to not quite know where she'll land next. For me, being surprised like everybody else is part of the magic of it."

Billie also attracted attention for the way she dressed: a wardrobe defined by layers of baggy clothing in a rainbow of loud colors. "I always wear the kind of stuff that makes you overheat and die," she joked to the *London Evening Standard*. Her first big purchase was an oversized yellow Tommy Hilfiger puffer coat, which she wore to the premiere of Netflix's *13 Reasons Why* (her song "Bored" was featured on the show's soundtrack). "I was so pumped. I thought it was the coolest thing in the world," Billie recalled to *Vogue* Australia. "I grew up with not a lot of money so I couldn't buy a bunch of shit I liked."

But everything changed once *dont smile at me* cracked *Billboard*'s Top 40 in 2018, not long after Billie's sixteenth birthday: Designers were gifting *her* clothing and jewelry, and Calvin Klein personally invited the stylish singer to sit in the front row at New York Fashion Week. She was even signed by Next Models for fashion and beauty endorsements. "Billie Eilish breaks boundaries in all that she does," founder Faith Kates said in a statement. "She is amongst the most influential musicians of her generation . . . The future is bright for Billie." But so was her present: Over the course of the year since she dropped *dont smile at me*, she went from playing to a crowd of five hundred to selling out all the dates of her global 1 by 1 Tour within two minutes.

Before hitting the road in October 2018, Billie sat down with *Vanity Fair* a second time for its "Time Capsule" video series. Twelve months prior, the magazine had brought in the up-and-comer for a Q&A—and the teen's rise to fame in that one year was staggering. Billie now boasted 6.3 million followers on Instagram, had played to forty thousand people at Atlanta's Music Midtown festival, and gushed about the most famous names in her phone: SZA, Miguel, Kaia Gerber, and *Stranger Things* star Millie Bobby Brown. Her fan base had also exploded, and the extra attention made it impossible to be a normal sixteen-year-old. Looking back at herself in 2017, "I'm kind of jealous of Billie a year ago," she confessed to *Vanity Fair*. "I don't know . . . I'm really not about to fucking pity myself for people recognizing who I am, because I'm really grateful for it. But, I don't know, I'd really like to go . . . anywhere."

POISED TO POP

In 2018, Billie scored a spot on *Forbes* 30 Under 30 list—four years before she was even twenty. The sixteen-year-old was recognized for her "social impact, revenue, funding, scale, inventiveness, and potential," and named one of music's stars on the rise in 2019, alongside genre-bending artist Post Malone, rappers Bad Bunny and 21 Savage, and former Fifth Harmony singers Camila Cabello and Lauren Jauregui. In celebration of Billie's honor, the magazine invited "the music sensation poised to pop" to its 30 Under 30 summit in Boston for a two-song performance ("bellyache" and "ocean eyes") and a sit-down interview in which she discussed how she made the leap from SoundCloud to a record deal with a major label. Just as *Forbes* predicted, 2019 was the year Billie exploded: Her debut full-length album, *WHEN WE ALL FALL ASLEEP, WHERE DO WE GO?* went straight to No. 1 on the charts and sold 1.2 million copies worldwide, tying with Lady Gaga's *A Star Is Born* soundtrack.

BEST NEW ARTIST

Billie had achieved worldwide fame before she even released an official album. When she and Finneas began the process of writing and recording her full-length debut, the stakes were higher—and so was the pressure. Whereas her label had been hands-off during the making of *dont smile at me*, now Darkroom imposed regular check-ins and a final deadline, which coincided with Billie's seventeenth birthday in December 2018. The stress started to seep into her subconscious, resulting in all-too-real nightmares and a recurring dream involving a creature that was a cross between a snake and the fictional xenomorph from the film *Alien*.

When she awoke, she'd draw it in a notebook. "This is literally how I got the whole concept for the album," she told *Rolling Stone* of WHEN WE ALL FALL ASLEEP, WHERE DO WE GO?, released in March 2019.

The creative process was just as monstrous, as Billie and Finneas pulled long nights in his bedroom studio. On the wall, next to where their heights were measured as children, the duo marked the progress of the album's fourteen songs. Over the doorway, Finneas scribbled another reminder, "10,000 Hours . . . ," the amount of time it takes to master a skill, according to best-selling author Malcolm Gladwell. There were definitely moments it felt never-ending and overwhelming, as fans got to see in the candid documentary *The World's a Little Blurry*, which came out more than two years later in 2021. Songwriting had always been Billie's least favorite part, and now she was overthinking every aspect of it—a situation that felt like "a minefield" to Finneas. "I've been told to write a hit, but I've been told to not tell Billie that we have to write a hit," he tells their mother, Maggie, in one scene. "I think she's terrified of anything she makes being hated. I think her equation is that the more popular something is, the more hate it's gonna get."

But it was nothing but love for the four singles they put out in the months leading up to the album's release—"you should see me in a crown," "when the party's over," "bury a friend," and "wish you were gay" all cracked the Top 40 of *Billboard*'s Hot 100. Still, the night before WHEN WE ALL FALL ASLEEP, WHERE DO WE GO? was set to drop, Billie had second thoughts. "Can we not put this out?" she asked her team backstage at a taping of *Jimmy Kimmel Live*. "I don't want to do it anymore." As she later explained to *Billboard* at the album's Spotify listening party, WHEN WE ALL

> *"I've been told to write a hit, but I've been told to not tell Billie that we have to write a hit."*

FALL ASLEEP felt like "my baby" and she just wanted fans to "cherish it" as much as she did. "I didn't want the world to be able to tell me how they feel about this thing I love . . . But the response has been crazy."

Crazy would be an understatement: *WHEN WE ALL FALL ASLEEP* debuted at No. 1 on the *Billboard* 200, making Billie the first artist born in the twenty-first century to top the chart. On streaming platforms, she notched 194 million on-demand plays in the first week, the third-biggest number ever for an album by a woman. Simultaneously with the album, she also dropped its fifth single, "bad guy," a nu-goth pop track with a catchy synthesizer riff that became the best-performing global hit of 2019— thus catapulting Billie into the mainstream. That year, the neon-haired

> "We made this album in a bedroom at our house that we grew up in and it was mastered in someone's living room, so it's really like anything is possible."

teen could be seen everywhere: on the covers of *Rolling Stone*, *Elle*, and *Vogue* Australia; performing on *Saturday Night Live* and *The Tonight Show Starring Jimmy Fallon*; and winning big at the American Music Awards, MTV Video Music Awards, and Teen Choice Awards. A week before her eighteenth birthday, Billie concluded her historic 2019 run being named both *Billboard*'s Woman of the Year and *Variety*'s Hitmaker of the Year. At the latter event, she shared the irony of *WHEN WE ALL FALL ASLEEP*'s mega-success. "When we were working on the album, somebody told me and my brother Finneas, my cowriter, that there was no hit on the album. I don't know what that was supposed to do, I don't know how that was supposed to help anyone—but that fool was wrong!"

And Billie proved it weeks later at the 2020 Grammy Awards, where she won five of her six nominated categories, including Album of the Year, Song of the Year ("bad guy"), and the coveted Best New Artist, beating out the exceptionally talented Lizzo, Lil Nas X, Rosalía, and Maggie Rogers. By the time she stepped onstage to accept her fourth award, Record of the Year for "bad guy," Billie was in tears and could only muster "thank you" as an acceptance speech. Backstage, she buried her face in Finneas's chest. "We made this album in a bedroom at our house that we grew up in and it was mastered in someone's living room, so it's really like anything is possible," she marveled to reporters in the pressroom.

But the night's biggest surprise was yet to come. In her dressing room, Billie's iPhone lit up with a FaceTime call from her childhood-crush-turned-friend, Justin Bieber. Documentary cameras captured the moment, as Billie gasped and covered her face. "Answer it," someone tells her as the teen squeals in excitement.

"Congrats . . . I'm so proud of you," Bieber gushed. "Where's your brother?"

"I have no pants on," replied Finneas from the next room.

"But it's Justin Bieber!" Billie exclaimed, as Finneas—who had won the Grammy for Producer of the Year—hurried over in his boxers.

At the age most young people are taking the SATs or going to prom, Billie was making music history, selling out world tours, and sweeping the Grammys. Her achievements were extraordinary—yet she often missed ordinary life, like driving around in the Dodge Challenger she got for her seventeenth birthday (a gift from her record label). "I feel like the things I'm missing out on are very, like, specific things that I always wanted to do," she admitted to *Vogue* in February 2020. "I always wanted to go get gas by myself. I always wanted to go get groceries for my mom." Once, Billie did successfully disguise herself to grab dinner out with friends, "and I hated it," she laughed. "It's not like I want to suddenly be somebody who isn't me and be anonymous. I want to be who I am and that means that I have to be this way and live this life. And I'm actually fine with that . . . I hope that doesn't come off as cocky. I hope that it comes off as grateful. I have an incredible life."

EVERYONE'S LITTLE SISTER

Throughout her journey in the music industry, Billie has had big brother Finneas by her side. But she also has a network of "sisters" who walked a similar path to stardom at a young age. Avril Lavigne was just eighteen years old when she topped the charts with "Complicated," and the pop-punk queen reached out to say she was always there to talk. "That made me break down," Billie confessed to *Billboard*. She also revealed ahead of her 2019 Coachella debut that she connected with Ariana Grande, who gained fame on Nickelodeon's *Victorious*. "We had this weird feeling for one another. Our careers are completely different and we're in different places, but we understand [one another]." Another child star, Selena Gomez, actually gave Billie one of her earliest opportunities, a spot on the soundtrack for her Netflix series *13 Reasons Why*. At the 2017 premiere, she introduced herself to the speechless singer, and the two have remained close, with Billie being invited to Selena's thirtieth birthday bash in 2022. The actress profoundly related to Billie's song "everything i wanted," about being famous and depressed. "She already knows of what this industry can be and become," Selena told Apple Music. "And when I heard that song, I just sobbed."

PURSUIT OF HAPPINESS

J ust as Billie reached the height of commercial success—a multiplatinum album, Grammys sweep, and sold-out world tour—COVID-19 forced her to take a step back in March 2020. What started out as a few weeks in lockdown snowballed into months, a period of self-reflection that encouraged the young artist to get to know herself on a deeper level, for better or worse. The previous summer, she had started seeing a therapist who helped her undo years of depression and dark thoughts. "I was thriving," Billie recalled to *Rolling Stone* in 2021. "I felt exactly like who I was. Everything around me was exactly how it was supposed to be. I felt like I was getting better. I felt happier than ever."

And part of the healing process was confronting the trauma, namely the people who put her through "some crazy shit," on her next album. Billie and Finneas had started working on new songs during the 2019 When We All Fall Asleep World Tour, so when the 2020 Where Do We Go? World Tour was postponed (and ultimately canceled) due to the ongoing pandemic, they made the most of the downtime. It was their mother Maggie's idea to ease back into the studio by meeting every Monday, Wednesday, and Thursday. Their first session, the duo knocked out "my future," an ambient ballad about loving oneself enough to walk away from a toxic partner. Three months later, Billie released it as a single—and the chart-topper proved her future was indeed bright. That fall, she took a break from recording to perform "my future" on the third day of the Democratic National Convention.

Two years on from the emotional nightmare that was *WHEN WE ALL FALL ASLEEP*, the singer embraced the creative process this time around. The biggest change was to her environment: from Finneas's tiny bedroom to the studio he built out in the basement of his brand-new home. Billie's mindset also expanded. "Before I always felt under pressure and anxious and felt like I wasn't doing enough right or doing a good job," she confessed in an interview with Vevo. "I felt like I wasn't very talented also at the time, and I actually feel much more confident in my craft now, and I feel I've worked really hard on that. This album was made in a very perfect time for me creatively. It was just so natural and easy and fun and calm."

Part of that was natural growth and maturity, as she aged out of her teen years. But more so, Billie credited weekly therapy sessions as a significant factor in her improved artistry. "It makes me not word-vomit and it makes me not have everything [in my head]," she explained to Apple

Music's Zane Lowe. "I talk through things in therapy that I don't even think about in my life, and then over the week, I'm like, 'wow that thing we talked about in therapy, I should write about that.'" Years of bottled-up emotions came pouring out, as she tackled childhood trauma ("Getting Older"), the price of fame ("NDA"), exploitation ("Your Power"), public opinion ("Therefore I Am"), and beauty standards ("Male Fantasy").

Billie named the album after her favorite track on it, "Happier Than Ever," a cathartic kiss-off to an ex (believed to be rapper Brandon "Q" Adams). "It's one of my most important songs I've ever written," she explained to NPR. "Do you ever want to say something to somebody for a really long time? You don't really know what you want to say or how to say it—and then maybe you have a conversation with somebody else, or you think a little bit about it, and you figure out what it is you've been trying to say for this entire period of time? That's how it felt: That was the entire writing process, that was the recording process. Everything involved in this song felt like how it feels when you finally find the words for something." Fans couldn't wait to hear what she had to say: In the weeks ahead of *Happier Than Ever*'s July 2021 release, the album set a record with 1.028 million pre-adds on Apple Music. It also became her second consecutive No. 1 on the *Billboard* Hot 100 chart—and all sixteen tracks landed on the Hot Rock & Alternative Songs chart.

Billie took the "Happier Than Ever" era literally, lightening her hair from black with neon green roots all the way to bleach blonde—which she showed off on the album's cover as well as the June 2021 issue of British *Vogue*. She also ditched her signature baggy clothing for uncharacteristic form fitting silhouettes, a makeover that evoked a shocking public reaction: a mix of backlash for being a "sellout" and creepy commentary on her figure. Billie just tuned out all the noise, explaining to NPR, "I wanted the theme of old Hollywood and beautiful and classy. It's just funny that people see new photoshoots and immediately think that you're a different person. I see people call me Blonde Billie—like, 'Blonde Billie said this, but Green Billie didn't say this.' And I'm like, what the hell? I'm not a category of a person. I'm the same person, for my whole life. I like this thing this time, and I like this thing that time."

Truthfully, she didn't care for "Blonde Billie" all that much: Within months, she was back to brunette. She later expressed regret over the hair color as well as the lingerie-clad British *Vogue* pictorial, neither of which was authentically Billie—thus causing a temporary identity crisis for the singer. "I'm trying to find myself again. I don't want to live the way that I lived last year," she confessed to *NME* in 2022, after *Happier Than Ever* was completely shut out of the Grammys, losing in all six of its nominated categories. "Before that, I was one kind of person and wore a certain type of clothes and made a certain type of music . . . and that haunted me, as people only thought of me in one dimension and I didn't like that."

Looking back at the blonde "happy" promo aesthetic, she admitted to *The Times*, "I don't know who that is, but that is not me! I didn't have any time to think. I just decided who I was. I just became that vibe. And I don't know if that was necessarily what I really was feeling. I was just grasping on to anything."

NEW HOLLYWOOD

The Los Angeles native took fans around the world on a tour of her Southern California hometown in *Happier Than Ever: A Love Letter to Los Angeles*, an innovative concert film that mixes live action and animation. The story follows Billie as she performs her 2021 album at the historic Hollywood Bowl amphitheater—backed by the Los Angeles Philharmonic orchestra—interspersed with vignettes of her cartoon self exploring local landmarks like the Roosevelt Hotel, Hollywood Forever Cemetery, and Hollywood Palladium theater on Sunset Boulevard. True to its name, *A Love Letter to Los Angeles*, directed by Robert Rodriguez and Disney animator Patrick Osborne, romanticizes the city à la Old Hollywood film noir. "It formed me, it made me who I am and gave me the opportunities that I got," Billie said on *Good Morning America*. "I don't think I'd have any of the same anything if it wasn't for my hometown. I owed Los Angeles some love." The Disney+ original felt the appreciation: *A Love Letter to Los Angeles* earned a Grammy nomination for Best Music Film.

GIRL, INTERRUPTED

At the age of twenty-one, Billie feared her music career was already over. Her second full-length album, *Happier Than Ever*, underperformed commercially compared to its record-breaking predecessor, *WHEN WE ALL FALL ASLEEP, WHERE DO WE GO?*, and as she worked on her third, self-doubt absolutely obliterated her creativity. "We'd been trying and it wasn't doing what it usually would do in me," Billie revealed during a *Hollywood Reporter* roundtable with fellow pop stars Dua Lipa and Olivia Rodrigo in 2023. "I was honestly like, 'Damn, maybe I hit my peak and I don't know how to write anymore?'"

Stuck in a "really, really dark place," a glimmer of light appeared via a FaceTime call from Academy Award–nominated director Greta Gerwig. She was working on the upcoming live-action *Barbie* film starring Margot Robbie as the iconic doll—and Gerwig wanted Billie to write the character's heart song. Immediately, Billie and Finneas were pulled out of their creative funk. The siblings had won an Oscar in 2022 for their James Bond theme song, "No Time to Die," proof that they were more than capable of delivering. After watching a rough cut of *Barbie* at Warner Bros., they sat down to write, and their impressions flowed out in a stream of consciousness. Within two hours, the sparse piano ballad "What Was I Made For?" was completed.

"Those first couple lyrics . . . just came right out," she recalled to Apple Music's Zane Lowe. It was a sentiment that mirrored her own professional stumble, yet Billie was initially oblivious to the connection. "I did not think about myself once in the writing process. I was purely inspired by this movie and this character and the way I thought she would feel, and wrote about that. And then, over the next couple days, I was listening and I was like, girl, how did this . . . honestly, and I really don't mean this to come off a conceited way at all, but I do this thing where I make stuff that I don't even know is . . . like I'm writing for myself and I don't even know it." Billie recorded a raw version and sent it to Gerwig via Voice Memos. "She basically was like, 'I've been weeping all day,'" Billie recalled to *Vanity Fair*. "I hadn't heard somebody use that word like that in a long time. But the rest is kind of history."

"What Was I Made For?" resonated far and wide, and was named one of the best songs of 2023 by *Variety*, *Billboard*, *The Hollywood Reporter*, and *Rolling Stone*. And during the 2024 awards season, it took home top honors

> "I did not think about myself once in the writing process. I was purely inspired by this movie and this character and the way I thought she would feel, and wrote about that."

at the Oscars, Grammys, and Golden Globes. Backstage at the Academy Awards in February, the two-time winner revealed to reporters how the *Barbie* experience impacted her next album: "We were just creative again. It woke us up and got us back on our thing and it was really special and powerful and I hold it deep and dear to my heart."

Fans finally got to hear "my favorite thing I've ever made" in May 2024 when Billie dropped *HIT ME HARD AND SOFT*, a collection of her ten most vulnerable songs to date. For the first time, she refrained from putting out any singles ahead of the album's release, explaining that each track required the context of the nine others. When lead single "LUNCH" did drop simultaneously with *HIT ME HARD AND SOFT*, her cryptic reasoning made a little more sense: It's about her sexual feelings for another girl.

"You hear [the songs] and you don't think, 'that's only about her life and she's the only one who can relate to that.' That's what's cool about music, it's for everyone."

"That song was actually part of what helped me become who I am, to be real," Billie confessed to *Rolling Stone*. "I wrote some of it before even doing anything with a girl, and then wrote the rest after. I've been in love with girls for my whole life." The singer didn't reveal her muse—or if the same person inspired her second single, "BIRDS OF A FEATHER," a breezy pop ballad about an everlasting love. However, three songs down the album's track list, "L'AMOUR DE MA VIE" ("The Love of My Life") is a dismissive kiss-off to a mystery ex.

Fans were quick to point out that *HIT ME HARD AND SOFT*—a title that references the extremes of Billie's personality—is so intimate that listening to it feels like reading the superstar's diary. However, Billie didn't believe she overshared at all. "I feel that way more when I talk," she explained to the UK's Capital radio station, "but in music, [the songs] are not so specific about my life—I mean, they are for me—but I think that you hear them and you don't think, 'that's only about her life and she's the only one who can relate to that.' That's what's cool about music, it's for *everyone*."

The universal appeal was evident in the numbers: HIT ME HARD AND SOFT received a half-billion global streams its first week, debuting at No. 2 on the *Billboard* 200, with all ten tracks charting on the *Billboard* Hot 100 as well. Critics heralded the album as "brilliant" (*Rolling Stone*), "ravishing" (*Los Angeles Times*), and "a marvelous maze of music" (*The Independent*). No one was more shocked by the warm reception than Billie. "It's been so good, I can't believe my eyes," she gushed to Capital. "It's better than I ever could have dreamed of in a million years."

But so was everything about her rise to fame, even if she didn't realize it at times. At twenty-two, she could finally experience the joy and reflect on her remarkable journey. "All I do is think about myself at twelve years old, and all the things I dreamed about and all the things I thought about," Billie revealed to Australian talk show *The Project* in 2024, as she prepared to embark on her sixth sold-out world tour. "I have literally gotten to live out, like, almost every single one of my dreams and that is so absolutely ridiculous. Every day of my life, I am just completely blown away."

BILLIE THE ACTRESS

The daughter of trained actors entered the family business in 2023 with a role in the Amazon Prime Video series *Swarm*, a Beyoncé-inspired satirical thriller about toxic superfan culture. Billie guest-starred in one episode as Eva, a manipulative female-empowerment cult leader who crosses paths with the main character Dre (Dominique Fishback) as she seeks revenge against online trolls who bashed her favorite pop star. The role was small, yet memorable—for fans and especially Billie, who enjoyed acting as a kid before she decided to focus on singing and dancing. The premise of *Swarm*, produced by actor-singer-rapper Donald Glover, obviously hit close to home for the world-famous pop star. "That fan passion is so real, and it's so beautiful, but it's also really scary," she told *Variety*. "And I think the show is a metaphor for this power—how people really are in the delusional nature of, 'She's gonna see me and we're gonna be best friends.' Fans are really, so powerful, and I think maybe they don't realize how powerful they are."

PART TWO

Stream Queen

DISCOGRAPHY

Billie Eilish went viral overnight in 2015 with her very first song, "ocean eyes"—and a decade later, she's accumulated more than eighty billion streams worldwide. On Spotify alone, she became the youngest artist to surpass one hundred million monthly listeners in 2024, at just twenty-two years old, and she is only the third artist in history to hit that milestone, behind Taylor Swift and The Weeknd, both of whom have recorded twice as many songs as Billie (eighty-two and counting). And it's only the beginning, despite being one of the most decorated singers in modern music. Billie and her songwriter-brother, Finneas, have just now hit their stride, she told *The Project*: "We started out so young and completely inexperienced, and now we're experienced. We know what we're doing finally."

DONT SMILE AT ME

INTRODUCING THE TWENTY-FIRST CENTURY'S POP ICON
RELEASE DATE: AUGUST 11, 2017

• TRACK LIST •

1. COPYCAT
2. idontwannabeyouanymore
3. my boy
4. watch
5. party favor
6. bellyache
7. ocean eyes
8. hostage

REISSUE BONUS TRACKS

9. &burn

EXPANDED EDITION BONUS TRACKS

10. lovely
(featuring Khalid)
11. bitches broken hearts

BEDROOM POP: Despite inking a major record deal with Interscope, Billie and Finneas recorded the EP in his bedroom studio at their family's home in Los Angeles, where they'd first made magic with "ocean eyes" in 2015. "We actually tried renting out a studio for a month," Billie revealed to MTV News, "but it was really hard there, and we ended up just doing it at home anyway." They utilized every square inch of the tiny space: Billie recorded vocals from the bed with a piano separating her from Finneas's cramped workstation of computer monitors and subwoofers. "There's a crazy intimacy to what we're doing," Finneas explained in a video tour for music label AWAL. "It's our house and it's where we live—it's where we've experienced everything."

RIOT GRRRL: The title of Billie's debut album is a nod to her feminist spirit—and individuality. "My EP is called *dont smile at me* for a lot of reasons, but one of them would be when [someone tells you], 'Smile. Why aren't you smiling? It's so much more beautiful when you smile,'" the teen explained to *Billboard*. "Everyone's taught to smile. Girls are like, 'Look happy, look like you're having fun!' I'm not gonna look like anybody except what I am . . . I like to be in control of how I look and how I feel and how I act and the obligation is to smile back at someone if they smile at you. Therefore, *dont smile at me*." At that time, in 2017, Billie wasn't a big fan of smiling in general (she still isn't)—and there's another reason why, she added: "I have an ugly little tooth."

ALL EYES ON BILLIE: The teen's first single was "ocean eyes," the same track that went viral overnight in November 2015, when Finneas uploaded it to SoundCloud. Although he originally wrote the dream-pop song for his band, "he thought it would sound really good in my voice," Billie explained to *Teen Vogue*. "He taught me the song and we sang it together along to his guitar and I loved it. It was stuck in [my] head for weeks." The earworm hit two million streams on SoundCloud yet had a slow burn when officially released on *dont smile at me*—and didn't crack the *Billboard* charts until Billie's next album, *WHEN WE ALL FALL ASLEEP, WHERE DO WE GO?*, in 2019.

One person who didn't initially get "ocean eyes" was Katy Perry, who revealed in 2023 that she had received an email years earlier about checking out a new artist named Billie Eilish to potentially sign to her label, Unsub Records (a record label under Universal Music Group). "It was a song called 'ocean eyes' and it was just a blonde girl and I was like 'Meh, boring.'" Katy recalled in a TikTok video posted by Los Angeles radio station 102.7 KIIS-FM. "Big mistake. Huge mistake." Looking around the room, she joked, "Don't let this hit the internet."

WHERE'S HER MIND: The second single, "bellyache," introduced a darker side of Billie's artistry, told from the perspective of a conflicted serial killer. But it didn't start out that way. Billie and Finneas were riffing in the garage one day when he blurted out a few lines about cruising around town with his friends, referring to them as "bodies." Billie took it in a different, fictional direction, with the "bodies" being corpses "because I just killed everyone," she explained to Junkee. "So then, that whole song we were just like, 'Okay, so this is about a psychopath, serial killer, bipolar, insane person, kind of.' Because it's also really childish, because it's a bellyache: No adult says, 'I've got a bellyache.'" How did she get into the mindset to write about such a topic? "Obviously I'm not a serial killer, I don't think, and so I just wrote about something that I'll never get to experience—but I can experience it in the song, which is almost more fun than killing people."

VISUALLY SPEAKING: Half the EP's tracks were turned into videos, cinematic productions that elevated the artistry of Billie's music. Lead single "ocean eyes" actually got two videos: the first focused on her singing alone in a purple haze, her own baby blues piercing through, while the second featured a choreographed group number that allowed Billie to showcase her dance talent—and has since netted more than 100 million views on YouTube. But the most popular video on Billie's channel from this era is for "bellyache," with 677 million views. In the visual, Billie is dressed in yellow and pulling a red wagon filled with garbage bags of money along a desert highway—until she finds the police waiting for her at the end of the road.

The least popular is "watch" (eighty-seven million views), a literal take on the song's lyrics about being burned by heartbreak. In the clip, Billie sets fire to "the old me," she explained to *Vice*. "The new me is kind of over it. So I go up to the old me like, 'Screw you, I'm going to light you on fire now.'" The final video, "hostage," shows off the singer's skills as a trained dancer, as she and her lover depict the demise of their relationship through choreography, both dressed in white in an equally colorless room. "hostage" earned Billie her first MTV Video Music Awards nomination for Best Cinematography, though the award ultimately went to Shawn Mendes and Camila Cabello for "Señorita."

BONUS TRACKS: *dont smile at me* was such a smash success, fans needed more than its eight songs. Four months after the EP's release, Billie reissued it with "&burn," a collaboration with rapper Vince Staples. The track is actually a continuation of "watch," originally titled "Watch & Burn," and follows Billie as she finally leaves the toxic relationship. An expanded edition of the EP added another two songs: "lovely," a ballad featuring Grammy-nominated singer Khalid that also appeared on Netflix's teen drama *13 Reasons Why*, and the R&B charmer "bitches broken hearts."

ON THE ROAD: In October 2017, Billie embarked on the Don't Smile at Me Tour, ten concerts around the US and in Toronto, Canada, at venues with capacities of several hundred people. The following February, she returned to the road with the Where's My Mind Tour, this time adding several stops throughout Europe. The setlist consisted of her EP's tracks, the new song "when the party's over," and a cover of Drake's "Hotline Bling," which Billie sang and performed on the ukulele with Finneas accompanying her on the acoustic guitar.

STREAMING SUCCESS: Despite not being a chart-topper, *dont smile at me* was considered a commercial hit at the time. But two years later, after Billie's mainstream success with *WHEN WE ALL FALL ASLEEP, WHERE DO WE GO?*, new fans rushed to stream her debut EP—and the teen became the youngest artist ever to hit one billion streams on Spotify in 2019.

WHEN WE ALL FALL ASLEEP, WHERE DO WE GO?

BILLIE'S MUSICAL DREAMS COME TRUE
RELEASE DATE: MARCH 29, 2019

• TRACK LIST •

1. !!!!!!!
2. bad guy
3. xanny
4. you should see me in a crown
5. all the good girls go to hell
6. wish you were gay
7. when the party's over
8. 8
9. my strange addiction
10. bury a friend
11. ilomilo
12. listen before i go
13. i love you
14. goodbye

JAPANESE EDITION BONUS TRACKS

15. come out and play
16. WHEN I WAS OLDER

JAPANESE LIMITED DELUXE EDITION BONUS TRACKS

17. bad guy (Remix)
(with Justin Bieber)

JAPANESE COMPLETE EDITION BONUS TRACKS

18. everything i wanted

DREAM DEBUT: Billie was clear she wanted to do "everything" on her debut album—and her wish came true in more ways than one. *WHEN WE*

ALL FALL ASLEEP, WHERE DO WE GO? blends pop with EDM, hip-hop, trap, R&B, alternative, and industrial genres. It all sounded good to fans, who helped catapult the album to No. 1 on the *Billboard* 200, with four of the seven singles receiving multiplatinum certification ("you should see me in a crown," "when the party's over," "bury a friend," and "bad guy"). Within three months, *WHEN WE ALL FALL ASLEEP* sold 1.3 million copies in the US alone. "The reaction was so surreal," Billie marveled to *Vanity Fair* in 2024. And when the album went on to win five Grammy Awards, "it was literally like the greatest thing that had ever happened to me, and I could not believe any second of it was real. That album really lives on for me. [It] completely changed my life."

NIGHTMARE SCENARIO: The album's title comes from a lyric in "bury a friend" and references some of the themes of *WHEN WE ALL FALL ASLEEP, WHERE DO WE GO?*: lucid dreaming, nightmares, and night terrors. The electronic-industrial song is written from the perspective of a monster living under someone's bed, which is hinted at in the cover art: Billie, with whited-out eyes and a demonic smile on her face, sitting on the edge of a bed in darkness. A sliver of light illuminates the singer, to appear like someone opened the bedroom door to find her like that. When she and Finneas wrote "bury a friend," "that's sort of when everything clicked in my head, and I just immediately knew what I needed everything about the album to be as like an overall theme, and just feeling," Billie explained to Apple Music's Zane Lowe. "The title I feel portrays exactly what I was trying to say with this whole album. The whole album is basically supposed to be a bad dream, or a good dream."

JUST THE BEGINNING: For many people, "bad guy" was their first time ever hearing of Billie Eilish, a teenager with a "cartoony" hit single that includes the line "duh." Despite the title, the lyrics are actually tongue-in-cheek. "It's basically making fun of everyone and their personas of themselves," she explained in an interview with Los Angeles radio station KIIS-FM. "I feel like you will never catch a bad bitch telling everyone she's a bad bitch. It's on—it's you. If you're going around all the time saying, like, 'Yeah, I'm bad, I'm always breaking rules and doing this and doing that.' You're not. I know that because I used to say that and I wasn't. Bad kids, bad boys, bad bitches, whatever, they do that shit and they don't even know."

"bad guy" proved good for the girl: The single peaked at No. 1 on the *Billboard* Hot 100, thus ending Lil Nas X's record-setting nineteen-week run with "Old Town Road." Elsewhere around the world, the single topped the charts in ten countries including Australia, Canada, and Greece. "I actually thought it would flop . . . because the chorus doesn't have a hook," Billie admitted to *Billboard*. "For some reason people do like it and it's huge now. It's one of my favorite songs I've ever made. It's my favorite to perform, it's so fun. I'm so proud of that song."

MADE FOR TV: Billie and Finneas found inspiration in all places, even some of their favorite television shows. "You should see me in a crown" is a direct quote from *Sherlock*, said by character Jim Moriarty in the second season, "and then we just wrote a song about being jiggy, I guess," Billie told the BBC. The chorus of "bad guy" borrows its sound from "Everything Is Not What It Seems," the theme song of Disney Channel's *Wizards of Waverly Place*, sung by the sitcom's star and Billie lover Selena Gomez.

"my strange addiction" is the title of a TLC reality show about odd behaviors, yet it includes soundbites from Billie's not-so-strange addiction: *The Office*. In an iconic 2011 episode of the NBC sitcom, "Threat Level Midnight," the characters make a movie starring Michael Scott (Steve Carell) as a secret agent named Michael Scarn, who has his own "Scarn dance." When Billie and Finneas came up with the beat for "my strange addiction," it reminded her of the song that plays during the Scarn dance. "I thought that was really funny, so we literally just ripped the audio from Netflix and put it in the song, not at all thinking that they would say yes to it and we'd be able to put it out," she told MTV News. Fortunately, *The Office* stars Carell, B. J. Novak (who wrote the episode), John Krasinski, and Mindy Kaling—whose voices are featured in the clip—all gave Billie their blessing.

BACK TO THE BEGINNING: The album ends fittingly with the two-minute "goodbye," comprised of a line from each of the previous twelve tracks, sung in reverse order. "That was Billie's idea, and I just thought it was really cool," Finneas told MTV. "The other thing I did was I layered in, really quietly, clips of all the songs on the album and played them backwards. To us, the motif would be when you grow up listening to a tape and at the end, you reverse the tape to go back to the beginning of the song."

IMMERSED IN THE SOUND: To celebrate the album's release, Spotify created an immersive experience in Los Angeles where fans could get acquainted with each song in a room filled with colors, smells, sounds, and feels associated with it—an ode to Billie's synesthesia, which enhances her

musical creativity. "I wanted it to literally be like an exhibit, a museum," she told *Billboard*. "Every room has a certain temperature, every room has a certain smell, a certain color, a certain texture on the walls. A certain shape, a certain number . . . I wanted to take my synesthesia and give it to the world and show everybody what it feels like."

ARENA TOUR: Billie took her debut album on the road with two appropriately titled world tours: When We All Fall Asleep World Tour (2019) and Where Do We Go? World Tour (2020). The first kicked off at Coachella and continued through three continents for a total of sixty-six shows, most played at theaters. Before it was even over, Billie announced the next one, her very first arena tour—which sold a half-million tickets within an hour of release. But after only three shows, in March 2020, she was forced to postpone the Where Do We Go? World Tour due to COVID-19, before ultimately canceling it altogether.

HAPPIER THAN EVER

AN ERA OF SELF-REFLECTION
RELEASE DATE: JULY 30, 2021

• TRACK LIST •

1. Getting Older
2. I Didn't Change My Number
3. Billie Bossa Nova
4. my future
5. Oxytocin
6. Goldwing
7. Lost Cause
8. Halley's Comet
9. Not My Responsibility
10. Overheated
11. Everybody Dies
12. Your Power
13. NDA
14. Therefore I Am
15. Happier Than Ever
16. Male Fantasy

GRIN AND BEAR IT: Despite its title, *Happier Than Ever* is anything but. In fact, "almost none of the songs on this album are joyful," Billie confirmed to *Rolling Stone*. Among the heavy topics she sings about: the downside of fame, emotional abuse, misogyny, mistreatment, mistrust, and loss of power—prompting Finneas to describe it as "a coping mechanism of an album."

Billie hoped fans going through similar experiences would be able to listen to songs like "Your Power," a dark ballad about an exploitive relationship, and "Lost Cause," which celebrates the end of a toxic romance, and find their own happiness. "The main thing that I would hope is, for people to hear what I say, and then go, 'Oh, God, I feel like that I didn't know that I felt like that. But this is how I feel,'" she explained in a Vevo interview. "I don't want to get too specific, because I think it's really for the listener to decide, I don't want to put the ideas into their brains, because I want them to feel a hundred percent that their own interpretation is the right interpretation."

TIMELESS CLASSIC: For her third collection of music, Billie toned down the tempo of her signature trap-electro-pop sound, with influences of jazz and the singers she grew up listening to like Frank Sinatra and Peggy Lee. "I wanted to make a very timeless record that wasn't just timeless in terms of what other people thought, but really just timeless for myself," she told Vevo. "And then the songs in the album are all over the place. And very versatile and different to one another, but also are very cohesive, which is like a big goal for me is to make things feel like the same project, but not like the same song over and over again."

IDENTITY CRISIS: A complete one-eighty from *WHEN WE ALL FALL ASLEEP*, Billie went blonde for the *Happier Than Ever* era, a polarizing makeover that divided fans—but more so, Billie herself. "At first it was fun. I was really excited for the blonde era, like, Blonde Billie is gonna be so cool. But it did not go how I wanted it to go," she admitted in a 2023 interview with the *Los Angeles Times*. "I completely had no idea who I was. I came up with this whole aesthetic, and I just got swallowed up into it."

HAPPY ENDING: "Happier Than Ever," about the end of an unhealthy relationship, was the first song Billie and Finneas wrote for the album, in the aftermath of her breakup from rapper Brandon "Q" Adams during the When We All Fall Asleep World Tour. Fans witnessed the volatile romance play out in her 2021 documentary, *The World's a Little Blurry*: In one haunting scene, Billie reveals to her best friend, Zoe Donahoe, that Q was in the emergency room with a broken hand after punching a wall in anger. Not long after, while in a tiny Denmark town, she and Finneas wrote the song's chorus on a kids guitar he had picked up for $80. "It just sounded really cute," he told *Billboard*. "We knew that we liked that idea, but we weren't in the period of time where we were like crunching down on an album, so we just put it in our back pocket and we'd write a line or two here and there."

"Happier Than Ever" was originally supposed to be the album's final track, until Billie wrote "Male Fantasy," which tackles the negative effects of beauty standards. Despite the song being "a hopeless realization and a horrible thing," she decided to make it the closer versus "Happier Than Ever" since "I just scream my lungs out," she told Spotify. "Not ending on an angry note, I think, was important because nothing should end on a bad note."

RISKY BEHAVIOR: As part of her self-reflection, Billie looked back on her overnight rise to fame and how it affected her personal relationships on "NDA" (which stands for nondisclosure agreement, a legal agreement popular with celebrities that restricts a person from sharing intimate details with the public). The song eschews the typical structure of verse-chorus-bridge-chorus-outro, which put Billie out of her comfort zone yet ultimately forced her to write one of her "coolest" songs.

For the music video, she took an even greater risk—two dozen professional drivers do donuts around her as she walks down a darkened road at night wearing all black. Billie came up with the death-defying idea and did all her own stunts, much to the horror of her mother who was on the set. In a behind-the-scenes clip Billie uploaded to Instagram, Maggie gasps and grabs her head as she watches the action from a safe distance.

KNOW PRESSURE: After the monster success of *WHEN WE ALL FALL ASLEEP*, naturally there were high expectations for its follow-up album. But instead of feeling pressure, Billie was emboldened by her record-smashing debut. "I wasn't worried; I was super confident," she revealed to NPR. "I really felt that I did the best that I possibly could have done with a second album: I didn't stay exactly doing the same thing, but I also didn't change into something else, I grew. I thought that that was really good." It wasn't until she started to put out promotional singles ahead of the album's release that she finally got nervous. "People are going to listen and tell me how they feel now? No! But, it's okay. It's really just about me liking it, and the real fans liking it. That's all I care about."

SHOW MUST GO ON: Two years after the Where Do We Go? World Tour was canceled after three shows due to the coronavirus pandemic, Billie returned to the road in 2022 with Happier Than Ever, The World Tour. The ten-month trek brought her through North America (including three cities in Mexico), South America, Europe, Asia, and Australia—and the eighty-eight concerts pulled in more than $131.7 million.

HIT ME HARD AND SOFT
THE TWO EXTREMES OF BILLIE EILISH
RELEASE DATE: MAY 17, 2024

• TRACK LIST •

1. SKINNY
2. LUNCH
3. CHIHIRO
4. BIRDS OF A FEATHER
5. WILDFLOWER
6. THE GREATEST
7. L'AMOUR DE MA VIE
8. THE DINER
9. BITTERSUITE
10. BLUE

THE OLD BILLIE: Three years after her blonde *Happier Than Ever* era, Billie got back to her old self with *HIT ME HARD AND SOFT*, a collection of personal songs that delved deep into her psyche. Looking back to 2019, the year she broke through with *WHEN WE ALL FALL ASLEEP, WHERE DO WE GO?*, it was the best time of her life; however, it was somewhat short-lived due to the COVID-19 shutdown in March 2020. Ever since, she found herself trying to get back "to the girl that I was. I've been grieving her," Billie confessed to *Rolling Stone*.

    Musically, she was resurrected on *HIT ME HARD AND SOFT*, a title that reflects the duality of her personality. While in the studio, she misunderstood the name of a synth in Logic Pro, the recording software used by Finneas, as "Hit Me Hard and Soft"—and realized it perfectly encapsulated the theme of the album, the two sides of Billie. "I'm a pretty extremist person, and I really like when things are really intense physically, but I also love when things are very tender and sweet," she explained to the magazine. "I want two things at once. So I thought that was a really good way to describe me."

GUESS WHO: In February 2024, Billie revealed her next album was complete and had already been mastered, the final step in the recording process, yet she stopped short of announcing a release date. Several weeks later, digital billboards with mysterious lyrics popped up around the world in Los Angeles, New York, Toronto, and Sydney. Fans knew immediately it was Billie, identifiable by her trademark Blohsh symbol, a gender-neutral stick figure, hidden in plain sight on the billboards. Another clue it was her: The singer changed her Instagram profile photo to an electric blue circle, the same shade of the lyrics—which turned out to be teases of her first single, "LUNCH."

EXPERIMENTAL ERA: As Billie explored her bisexuality in her personal life, she sang about it for the first time on "LUNCH," which is about a girl who looks good enough to taste, both in the literal and figurative sense. The track was also musically experimental, leaning into electro, synth, pop, rock, and post-punk genres—and ultimately soared to the top of a wide variety of *Billboard* charts (Adult Pop, Dance, Hot Rock & Alternative, Pop, and Rock). And she was hungry for more. On the heels of "LUNCH," Billie collaborated with fellow pop star Charli XCX on a remix of her *Brat* track, "Guess," praised as "super-sapphic" by LGBTQ+ newspaper *PinkNews*. In Billie's verse, she fantasizes about the color of Charli's underwear—and in

the video, she's surrounded by ten thousand pairs of panties (all of which were donated to charity).

NEW HEIGHTS: The singer hit the highest note of her career in "BIRDS OF A FEATHER," also her most romantic song to date. Toward the end, she belts out a D5 note and it was her proudest moment during the making of *HIT ME HARD AND SOFT*. Alone in Finneas's home recording studio, she was trying out different versions of the lyric's harmony, and with each note she successfully reached, she told herself, "Dude, I'm gonna have to keep going . . . I got this one, I'm just gonna hit the higher one," Billie happily recalled to Apple Music's Zane Lowe. "I could not belt until I was literally eighteen. I couldn't physically do it." She was so ecstatic that she finally could, she drove straight to her parents' home to tell her mom.

In the same interview with Lowe, Finneas revealed that he purposely taught Billie how to record her vocals because he knew there were certain things she would not attempt to try unless alone in the studio. "I think that really shines on the album: A person, even without their collaborator in the room, doing the bravest thing ever."

POLARIZING VISUAL: The *HARD AND SOFT* singer is pulled in different directions, literally, in the music video for "BIRDS OF A FEATHER." The visual opens with Billie sitting in an empty office when an invisible force drags her around the work space—and right through walls!—yet she's too smitten to notice the chaos. Some fans expressed disappointment in the premise, explaining they were expecting something a little more serene with flowers and, well, birds.

DEEP END: The album's cover art is as deep as *HIT ME HARD AND SOFT*'s lyrical content. In the image captured by underwater photographer William Drumm, Billie is seemingly drowning after falling through an open door that's floating on the surface. It looks like something out of a nightmare, and according to the singer, that's exactly how it felt throughout the "brutal" six-hour shoot as she remained submerged in a tank of water with a ten-pound weight strapped across her chest (under her clothing). In between each attempt to get the underwater shot, Billie clung to a flotation device on the surface and received additional oxygen from a mask for thirty seconds. Then she would hold her breath for two minutes, as two men literally dragged her down ten feet to the bottom of the tank—over and over again.

"I didn't have any nose plugs and I also had my eyes open," she told Los Angeles radio station 102.7 KIIS-FM. "I've got to say the eyes open underwater for six hours was one of the most intense pains I've ever experienced." The cover image is of Billie's profile with her head facing up toward the door, so without nose plugs, "I was basically waterboarding myself for six hours, with my eyes open. I worked so hard and I got the shot, and it's so good, but it was hell!"

HARD NUMBERS: *HIT ME HARD AND SOFT* was so highly anticipated, fans helped Billie set a new personal record on Spotify: 72.7 million streams in a single day, her biggest debut on the platform. Within the first week, the album reached 500 million streams—and in less than two months, she surpassed the 2 billion mark. In addition to its commercial success, *HARD AND SOFT* was a winning combo to the Recording Academy: Billie received six 2025 Grammy nominations, including Album of the Year, Best Pop Vocal Album, and Song of the Year for "BIRDS OF A FEATHER," but she was snubbed in all categories.

AUDIENCE PARTICIPATION: Hit Me Hard and Soft: The Tour kicked off in September 2024 and continued through the following summer, stopping in seventy cities across North America, Europe, and Australia. Billie electrified fans the first night in Quebec City when she rocked out on a Fender Telecaster guitar during "Happier Than Ever." She also requested a moment of total silence from the sold-out crowd of eighteen thousand while she gave them a peek at her music-making process: Sitting cross-legged centerstage she recorded herself singing "when the party's over" so she could play it back on a loop to harmonize with her live voice for the performance. By the end of the night, the singer's long hair was such a knotted mess, her ponytail holder was stuck in her hair—and she hopped offstage so fans in the front row could try to untangle it.

PART THREE

Billie Bossa Nova

BILLIE A TO Z

Billie is as colorful as her once-signature neon hair: A two-time Academy Award winner who has been the face of both Nike and Gucci and can whip up a vegan meal as skillfully as she can entertain a sold-out crowd of 250,000. Whether you're a longtime Eyelash who's been around since the SoundCloud days or late to the party (don't worry, it's never over, despite the title of her 2018 hit single), there's always something new to learn about the musical powerhouse. Check out the A (Air Force 1) to Z (childhood bestie Zoe) of the one and only Billie Eilish!

AIR FORCE 1

It was a match made in sneakerhead heaven when Billie announced her partnership with Nike in 2021. After releasing two popular styles of Air Jordans, the singer stepped it up with the Billie × Nike Air Force 1 Mushroom, a modern take on the classic shoe. Light brown in color, the eco-friendly vegan's high-top is synthetic nubuck made of recycled materials and features five chunky mid-foot straps, capturing her signature oversized style. Six months later, in November 2022, to coincide with the fortieth anniversary of the Air Force 1, she dropped the Billie Eilish AF1 Low, in both Mushroom and Sequoia (slate gray) colorways, using leftover material waste from production of her AF1 High. "I want my collaboration with Nike to tell a story that not only highlights the importance of recycling but also reminds us that we need to take better care of our planet," Billie stated.

In 2023, she rolled out the triple-white Billie AF1 Low and introduced a new line, Billie × Nike Air Alpha Force 88, inspired by the vintage 1980s shoe that Michael Jordan wore before designing his own. Available in five colorways—nicknamed Triple Red, Fire Red (white-red-black), White Black, Game Royal (white-blue-black), and Venom Green—the synthetic leather shoe features a padded textile collar and adjustable forefoot strap. Billie branding decorates the sockliner, as well as the box and even its tissue paper, making the Billie x Nike Air Alpha Force 88 ($130) the ultimate collectible for fans—but also a must-have for discerning streetwear fanatics.

BLOHSH

How many singers can say they have their very own logo? Billie's is a gender-neutral stick figure that's slightly skewed, known as Blohsh—what

> "I want my collaboration with Nike to tell a story that not only highlights the importance of recycling but also reminds us that we need to take better care of our planet."

it would sound like if you said "Billie Eilish" really fast. Since 2016, the graphic emblem has popped up everywhere from music videos and billboards to T-shirts, hats, face masks, and even blankets. It's so significant to Billie, she wore a custom silver Blohsh pendant necklace on one of the biggest nights of her young career, the 2020 Grammy Awards when she swept the four major categories. Fans can snag a similar version in blue on her website ($60), as well as a Blohsh die-cut dog tag ($75).

Blohsh, which inspired its own Instagram account, has become so synonymous with Billie, Google actually swapped its own Pegman for her unisex icon in 2024 during the singer's Hit Me Hard and Soft: The Tour. Any fan using Google Maps near the concert venue could open the app and navigate to Billie's favorite plant-based restaurants or her recommended fuel-efficient routes, following the Blohsh on Street View.

> *"Nobody ever knew it wasn't me, literally nobody knew."*

COACHELLA

Billie had never even attended the iconic music festival until she was on the 2019 bill. The seventeen-year-old played the second night and kicked off her fifteen-song set with the high energy "bad guy" before working through her most popular tracks, including "you should see me in a crown," "bellyache," "ocean eyes," and "bury a friend." There were a few technical difficulties—a malfunction with the LED-paneled floor delayed the set thirty minutes, special guest Vince Staples's mic wasn't on during "&burn," and Billie forgot the lyrics to "all the good girls go to hell." But she wasn't fazed, describing the overall experience as "life-changing" on Instagram.

Three years later, she made a triumphant return to Coachella—this time as a headliner. Billie's performance was twenty-five songs, stretched across an A-stage, B-stage, and acoustic interlude. But it's how it began that got people buzzing: During the light-show introduction, fans caught a quick glimpse of Billie onstage before she suddenly popped up in the middle of the crowd, wrapped in a ginormous puffer coat. "I had a body double, one of my dancers from the show," she confessed to Apple Music's Matt Wilkinson. "I dressed her up in a show look that I had worn before. We got a black wig and we put buns in it and we gave her a mask and sunglasses and she wore my shoes and my socks. Nobody ever knew it wasn't me, literally nobody knew. And while she's up there, I put on a big black coat and like a traffic vest and a hood and just glasses. And I walked *through* the crowd, all the way out to the end of the thrust [stage]. Got under the thrust, took it all off, and got on and started the show. It worked!"

DYE JOBS

The natural blonde has experimented with just about every color of the rainbow: neon red, acid green, electric blue (which faded to a teal), pale purple, chocolate brown, jet black, rose gold, gray, and—for one short week—copper red, while transitioning from blonde to brunette. When she got her driver's license in 2019, Billie was rocking her signature green roots, a hair color defined as "other" by the DMV on her official card.

Over the evolution, there have been some misadventures. In 2018, after the wrong toner accidentally turned Billie's white hair "lavendery-blue," she leaned into the blue, despite it being her least favorite color. Unfortunately, the stylist had used a permanent dye. "That shit is not coming out," she dished to Buzzfeed at the time. "I have sat in that stupid salon chair for hours, and hours, and hours . . . and that bitch will not get the fuck out of my hair." Ultimately, she had to dye it all black

to cover up the botched blue hue. Then when Billie first experimented with two-tone hair in 2019, the person who did it "burned half of it off," she admitted to TMZ when asked about her new "mullet" cut. "I'm growing that shit out."

To coincide with *Happier Than Ever* in 2021, she lightened up with platinum blonde, a jaw-dropping makeover that broke an Instagram record with one million likes in six minutes. But as it took four marathon bleach sessions to achieve, and just as much effort to maintain, Billie went back to black in 2022—and has preferred the dark side ever since.

EYELASHES

Every devoted fanbase has their own special name, and Billie's faithful following is up there with Swifties, Little Monsters, Arianators, and the Beyhive. In 2017, the singer dubbed her diehards "Eyelashes" during an appearance on MTV's *TRL*. Since the very beginning, Billie has shared an especially close relationship with fans—many as young as herself— whether connecting over social media or recognizing them in the crowd at concerts or public appearances. "I feel like it's such a passion and the fact that people feel that way about me is so insane," the fifteen-year-old told *Harper's Bazaar* back in 2017. "It's really special for me. I don't like to call them my fans because they're my family; they're the only reason I'm anything . . . I spend as much time with them as I can and make connections with them 'cause they're people."

Billie has had the opportunity to surprise some of her biggest Eyelashes with elaborate ruses—and it's hard to tell who's more touched by the experience. A young girl named Dakota thought she was testing out the "bad guy" moves on *Just Dance 2020* and opened up about how Billie's music helped her deal with not having friends, unaware her favorite singer was listening. When she turned around to see Billie, she burst into tears. "You're so beautiful," Billie told the pigtailed Dakota, embracing her in a hug. "I love you." In the UK, sixteen-year-old superfan Marissa was brought on the *Capital Breakfast* radio show under the auspice of sharing how she juggles school while also caring for her disabled mother and little brother. It was Billie who fought back tears as she sat down next to Marissa and heard how her songs got the brave teen through the darkest times.

Several lucky Los Angeles–based fans have run into Billie at red lights, and in viral videos of these run-ins, she's always happy to roll down the window for a quick chat. During a 2024 appearance on *Jimmy Kimmel Live*, the host played a clip from the last time she had been on the show and was swarmed by Eyelashes as she drove off the Hollywood lot. Kimmel couldn't believe Billie hit the brakes to talk to the fans—let alone that she recognized them. "What's been so cool is that all of these fans, my little family, we've been growing up at the same time," she explained. "When I was first starting out, there would be certain kids I would see at every thing I would do, and we were all the same age . . . over the years, I've seen the same faces multiple times—there's some here [in the audience], there's some outside—and I recognize them obviously because I'm a person with eyes," she joked. "It's so special, it feels like seeing my old friend again."

FRAGRANCES

Billie's three signature fragrances smell just like her music sounds: harmonious, alluring, and tantalizing. The singer got into the lucrative celebrity perfume market in 2021 with Eilish, her "favorite smell in the world": notes of vanilla, soft spices, cocoa, red berries, and musk.

"Over the years, I've seen the same faces multiple times . . . It's so special, it feels like seeing my old friend again."

To complement the amber scent, the bottle is a bronze bust of a woman (however, the fragrance is unisex). "I've always had an infatuation with back and collarbones and just like, bones and bodies," Billie explained to *Vogue*. She stuck with the same design (in black) and name for Eilish No. 2, an earthy blend of bergamot, apple blossom, black pepper, and palo santo. In 2023, Eilish No. 3 joined the collection (in red) as a limited-edition fragrance that opens with grapefruit, pink peppercorn, and jasmine and then unfolds into saffron, fresh fir needles, and creamy cedar.

Creating her own fragrance was a lifelong dream for Billie, who collected perfume bottles as a kid. Her first two scents—projected to generate more than $120 million in sales, according to *Forbes*—were

"I am honored to be part of Gucci's evolution in rethinking tradition"

inspired by childhood memories: baking with her mother (No. 1) and the smell of a sidewalk after the rain (No. 2). Originally available online via billieeilishfragrances.com and ulta.com (but now everywhere), No. 1 and No. 2 sold out within minutes, "which is truly just the power of Billie and her fan base," Lori Singer, president of Billie's fragrance distributer Parlux, told *WWD*. "When we did enter brick-and-mortar with Ulta as our exclusive partner, we overachieved our launch volume by 100 percent. Our goal is to build Billie Eilish fragrances into a fragrance house that will be a true and enduring pillar in the industry."

GUCCI

One iconic logo has been seen again and again on Billie's clothing since the very beginning of her career: the interlocking Gs of Gucci. After years of repping the Italian fashion house on red carpets, in 2021, she collaborated with creative director Alessandro Michele on limited-edition vinyl box sets of *Happier Than Ever*, done in psychedelic patterns with matching Gucci nail-art stickers included. The following year, Billie was the star of Gucci's second eyewear collection, three distinct retro styles she modeled in a high-art campaign inspired by Old Hollywood.

It was her third Billie × Gucci collaboration that made the eco-friendly singer the proudest: In 2023, she introduced Gucci's Horsebit 1955, which is their first bag to be crafted in an animal-free material called Demetra, which took the luxury brand two years to develop and is made with 75 percent plant-based raw materials. "I am honored to be part of Gucci's evolution in rethinking tradition," Billie told *Vogue*. "It's a new understanding, and one that isn't afraid to evolve in a new direction, that truly matters to me."

HIGHLAND PARK

The Los Angeles suburb is where Billie was born and raised, entrenched in a vibrant artistic and multicultural community of all socioeconomic backgrounds. Just a few tree-lined blocks from the O'Connell family home is one of Highland Park's main drags, York Boulevard, a trendy stretch of artisan bakeries, coffee shops, boutiques, and cafes. "[It's] kinda where everything is," Billie explained to *Coup de Main* magazine. "It's kinda like a little hipster block party, almost."

When her parents Patrick and Maggie bought their quaint 1912 bungalow back in 2001—just four months before Billie was born—Highland Park had not yet been gentrified; therefore it was affordable for the young family. "It's a great neighborhood and nobody really lived there," Billie told

the magazine in 2017. "It wasn't a popular place at all, then over time, tons of stores and little shops popped up, and it's huge now, and kinda popping, which is weird. I think it's really cute. It's very homely, very comfortable."

Billie is so attached to Highland Park, she continued to live with her parents in their two-bedroom home through her early fame until 2019, when she bought a $2.3 million horse ranch just ten miles away in Glendale, a mountainous LA suburb. Still, the teen pop star often returned to spend the night in her childhood bedroom—sometimes with a bodyguard sleeping in the living room, after the address leaked online. "It was really traumatizing," she told *Rolling Stone*. "I completely don't feel safe in my house anymore, which sucks. I love my house."

INK COLLECTION

"I *love* tattoos," Billie declared in a 2021 interview with *Vanity Fair*. "My mom hates tattoos." Shortly after the singer turned eighteen, she got her first—and for a worthy reason. To commemorate sweeping the 2020 Grammy Awards (winning all four of the major categories), Billie got inked with an everlasting homage to herself: "Eilish" tattooed across her chest in an ornate gothic font. "Yes, I love myself," she joked to *VF*. And the ink is for her eyes only: "You won't ever see it," she teased fans. However, we did get a peak at the singer's second tattoo, a massive dragon that stretches from her thigh to her stomach, when she wore a sheer nude corset in the June 2021 issue of British *Vogue*. Billie has yet to reveal its meaning, but coincidentally she named her first car, a matte black Dodge Challenger, Dragon. Another kind of mythical creature graces her left hand: three "sweet little guardian angel fairies" from her favorite childhood book, *Fairyopolis*, she told *VF*.

Despite the air of mystery surrounding her tattoos, Billie gave her Instagram followers a behind-the-scenes peek at an October 2023 session with artist Matias Milan, aka "Beer Spill," who specializes in sigilism, a modern type of tribal design popular in the 1990s. In the photo Billie uploaded, the singer's ink is abstract and hard to decipher, but it's massive and runs from the nape of her neck down her entire spinal column. Her fifth tattoo needs no explanation: "Hard Soft," in honor of her 2024 album, *HIT ME HARD AND SOFT*, in cursive on her left hip.

JAMES BOND

At seventeen, Billie became the youngest artist ever to record a James Bond theme song, "No Time to Die," which she and Finneas wrote for the 2020 film of the same name. The haunting track, composed by Academy Award winner Hans Zimmer and backed by a seventy-person orchestra, reflects the emotion of the spy flick's story, a web of betrayal and revenge for James Bond (Daniel Craig). The project was a dream come true for the siblings, so much so that when they sat down to write the 007 theme, they had zero ideas. On tour at the time, Finneas set up a mini-studio in their green room, and during a stop in Texas, he finally came up with the opening chord—and rushed to share it with Billie, who was in the middle of a meet and greet with fans. Once she heard it, she was able to craft the vocal melody, and then together, Billie and Finneas wrote lyrics based on the one scene they were given by the *No Time to Die* producers.

To add even more pressure, it was Craig's final film as Bond—and the actor had final approval of his swan song. When he first listened to "No Time to Die," he wasn't convinced it "delivered the right emotional climax," producer Stephen Lipson revealed to *Music Week* magazine. "I asked

Finneas and Billie to give me a climactic vocal moment which Billie wasn't too sure about, but when I heard it I knew it would deliver." After some final mixing, Lipson played the track for Craig. He didn't look up once, and when it ended, he asked to hear it again. After the second spin, "he looked up at me and said something like, 'That's fucking amazing.'" The critics agreed: "No Time to Die" won a Grammy, Oscar, and Golden Globe.

KATY PERRY'S FINACÉ

One of the lighter moments in Billie's documentary, *The World's a Little Blurry*, is when she met Katy Perry before performing at Coachella in 2019. The "Firework" pop star gushed about being a big fan and introduced Billie to her fiancé Orlando Bloom, who "plays 'bad guy' all of the time." The actor was just as excited as Katy, hugging Billie and telling her "how proud" he was of her. Back in her trailer, Finneas jokingly impersonated his English accent, prompting Billie to ask, "Who was that?" Her brother then pulled up photos of Bloom's character in *Pirates of the Caribbean* and completely blew her mind. "That was him? No way! Bring him back! I wanna meet him again. He kissed me on the cheek! I did not know that was him. I thought that was just some dude Katy Perry met."

Billie got a second chance with Bloom before she hit the stage. Just as the show was about to start, the handsome actor passed by on his way to the restroom—and stopped to embrace the singer and give her a few more words of encouragement. "This is the universe hugging you," said Bloom, as he rocked Billie back and forth. "I'm giving you so much love and light right now."

"You don't even understand," she told him. "My nine-year-old self, bro . . . Oh my lord. Thank you for everything you do. I love you."

LIVE AT THIRD MAN RECORDS

On November 6, 2019, Billie played a secret acoustic show in Nashville at Jack White's Third Man Records—but fans who didn't score an invite still got to experience the magic. The eleven-song performance was recorded direct to acetate and released weeks later on vinyl, *Live at Third Man Records*. The packaging was just as exclusive: blue opaque vinyl. And for those lucky enough to snag a limited-edition copy, the sleeve featured a one-of-a-kind splatter of blue paint created by Billie herself. Originally only available at two Third Man stores in Nashville and Detroit, the live album was made available internationally on Record Store Day in 2020, making it the No. 1 release at independent music stores, outselling Taylor Swift, David Bowie, Metallica, and Tyler, The Creator.

MURAKAMI

Billie linked up with one of the most influential contemporary artists, Takashi Murakami, for a collaboration that spanned music and merchandise. The teen had wanted to work with Murakami, so she decided to reach out via Instagram, only to discover he had already sent her more than a dozen messages, none of which she had seen. "He was just like, 'I love everything you do,'" she revealed at a 2019 Adobe Max keynote discussion with Murakami. "My mind was blown." Soon after, Billie flew to Tokyo and the two met at his studio, where they envisioned the creative direction for her video for "you should see me in a crown," which Murakami directed. Using motion-capture technology, he turned Billie into a purple-haired anime character decked out in an oversized neon green t-shirt and shorts who dances around a psychedelic world, until she morphs into a monster and terrorizes his iconic smiling rainbow flowers.

> "Murakami is an incredible visionary. It was such an honor to collaborate with him and have our brains and our worlds collide for this ['you should see me in a crown'] video."

"Murakami is an incredible visionary," Billie said in a press release. "It was such an honor to collaborate with him and have our brains and our worlds collide for this video." And they didn't stop there. In 2020, Billie and Murakami kept the creativity flowing for a Uniqlo apparel collection that blended her Blohsh logo with the Japanese artist's manga-style motifs.

NET WORTH

At eighteen, Billie was the youngest person on the *Forbes* Celebrity 100 list when she made her debut in 2020 (at No. 43, notably several spots ahead of Kim Kardashian and Drake). Worth an estimated $53 million, the singer's wealth is a combination of record sales, streaming revenue, touring, merchandise, endorsements, and other ventures. In 2021, she reportedly

earned a $1 million advance for her photography book, *Billie Eilish*. That same year, her documentary, *The World's A Little Blurry*, was released on AppleTV+, an exclusive deal that paid $25 million according to *Forbes*.

In August 2024, Billie took the title of Spotify's most streamed monthly artist with 105 million listeners on the platform, which pays out $0.003 to $0.005 per play of a song. At the time, her music catalog was nearing 40 billion total streams on Spotify—equivalent to at least $117 million in revenue (which is then divvied up between Billie, Finneas, their record labels, musicians, and engineers who worked on the tracks). Another big chunk of Billie's net worth comes from concert ticket sales: after canceling the Where Do We Go? World Tour in 2020 due to COVID-19, two years later, her sold-out Happier Than Ever, The World Tour pulled in $131.7 million.

OBSESSIONS

When Billie loves something, she loves it hard (and soft). And many of her favorite things have remained the same over the years, making her an unexpected creature of habit when it comes to go-to foods, favorite television shows, and celebrity crushes. Billie's obsession with Justin Bieber is well-documented—a video of the moment she met him in 2019 became a viral sensation—but as a kid, she would watch his music video for "As Long As You Love Me" on repeat "and just sob," she admitted on *me & dad radio*, an Apple Music podcast she hosted with her father, Patrick (and occasionally her mother). "We did consider taking you to therapy," added Maggie, "because you were in so much pain over Justin Bieber."

Day in and day out, "I'm watching something," Billie confessed to *Variety*, "and it's normally *The Office*." She's seen all nine seasons of the

> *"She does it on a level we've never experienced, but I just feel such a love towards her and her family."*

NBC comedy series starring Steve Carell so many times—she estimates at least thirty—"I have all the scenes memorized." The show is such a comfort to Eilish that she will play an episode on her phone, turn it over, and use the audio as white noise when she's home. During the COVID-19 lockdown, she binged old favorites *New Girl*, *Jane the Virgin*, and *Sherlock*, and discovered new obsessions, such as the thrillers *Killing Eve* and *The Flight Attendant*, and watched the 2020 feminist film *Promising Young Woman* "like four times."

Billie's ultimate comfort is, like, so relatable. She once tweeted, "food is such a powerful little hoe," and during a 2019 appearance on the YouTube talk show *Hot Ones*, she revealed what meal compelled her to make such a statement: a Taco Bell bean burrito (no cheese). The vegan singer even took her Instagram followers along through a drive-thru—and shockingly ordered *twenty* bean burritos "with only beans, nothing else." Despite a gluten sensitivity that sometimes gives her a stomachache, Billie embraced a new food obsession in 2024: "a lot of bread."

PARAMORE

So many musical artists have taken Billie under their wing, but there's one whom she got to also take under hers: Paramore singer Hayley Williams. The two were admirers of each other from afar, and when they finally met, it was the beginning of a beautiful friendship. In 2022, as the rock band was working on its comeback album, *This Is Why*, Billie brought out Williams as a surprise guest for her headlining set at Coachella. The talented ladies brought down the house with an acoustic duet of Paramore's breakthrough hit, "Misery Business"—which came out in 2007 when Billie was five. Still, her Gen Z fans knew all the words to the pop-punk millennial anthem. In a passing-of-the-torch moment, Williams returned to the stage for Billie's finale, "Happier Than Ever," specifically the acoustic-to-rock transition when the two head-banged, famously Williams's signature move. They did it again the following July when Billie came out to sing her "all-time favorite" Paramore song, "All I Wanted," at the band's Los Angeles concert.

Just like Billie, the Paramore frontwoman was only fourteen when she got signed by a major record label. The first time she saw an interview with Billie, "I felt like there was something inside of me that was watching me . . . navigating this world," Williams told SiriusXM in 2022. "She does it on a level we've never experienced, but I just feel such a love towards her and her family, and I think they're so special. I went to their house last year for Thanksgiving, had some really great vegan cinnamon rolls that her mom Maggie made . . . the rest is history."

QUEEN OF GEN Z POP

Born just thirteen days before the end of 2001, Billie is officially a member of Generation Z (1997–2012), the era after millennials (1981–1996) and before Generation Alpha (2013–2025). Famous long before she even learned how to drive, she's the first global superstar born in this millennium. And she has the accolades to prove it: Billie is the first artist born in the twenty-first century to have a number-one hit single ("bad guy") and an Academy Award (Best Original Song, "No Time to Die").

Of course, her influence goes far beyond music. As one of the generation's leading (and loudest) voices, she is quintessential "Z": socially conscious, transparent about mental health, tech-savvy, pragmatic, and undeniably individualistic. The world might be a difficult place for her sometimes, but she's devoted to protecting the planet for future generations by prioritizing sustainability in all aspects of her career (prohibiting the sale of single-use water bottles on tours and selling merchandise made from recycled materials), inspiring a whole generation to be mindful of their own footprint. "People underestimate the power of a young mind that is new to everything and experiencing for the first time," the seventeen-year-old explained to *NME* in 2019. "We're being ignored and it's so dumb. We know everything."

Also known as iGen, Gen Z is the first to be "digitally native"—they don't know a world without cell phones and the Internet. The digital age has shaped their everyday life, for better or worse. For Billie specifically, it's a significant part of her daily routine. "I can't go to the bathroom without watching something on my phone," she told *Rolling Stone* in 2021. "I can't brush my teeth. I can't wash my face." However, while operating a mobile device is instinctive, laptop computers are straight out of the

> *"People underestimate the power of a young mind that is new to everything and experiencing for the first time. We're being ignored and it's so dumb. We know everything."*

dark ages. "I never learned to type because I wasn't that generation," she admitted to *RS* in 2024, "and now I regret it."

RESCUE DOG

When the COVID-19 lockdown postponed her 2020 world tour, Billie decided to do something constructive with her forced downtime at home: she fostered puppies. Finneas had previously adopted a dog from Angel City Pit Bulls, a rescue organization in Los Angeles, so Billie gave them a call and days later, two five-week-old, dark-gray pit bull pups in need of a home showed up at hers. "I fostered them over the summer, and then of course COVID started to grow, and meanwhile, I fell in love with the puppies," she told *Vogue* in 2024. Billie was especially smitten with

the male, "a little lug" with a goofy overbite who she named Shark, and eventually decided to keep him (a family friend adopted the other pup). "I just loved his color and I loved his personality. He's got these human eyes for sure, and I could picture my life with him."

Indeed, the two are inseparable: Shark goes everywhere with Billie, even the recording studio where he has a friend in Finneas's pit bull, Peaches. Shark is so unaffected by loud music that he typically snores through sessions—which Billie captured on "The Greatest" from *Hit Me Hard and Soft*. And when she previewed the album at the Kia Forum in LA, her four-legged son joined her onstage. "I wish that I could take him everywhere with me," she told *Vogue*. "I wish I could take him on my whole tour across the world."

SYNESTHESIA

There's a scientific reason why Billie is as much of a visual artist as she is a musical artist. The singer has synesthesia, a sensory crossover that allows her to literally see her music, as her mind associates everything with a color, number, shape, smell, and texture. For example, "bad guy" is yellow and red (prominent colors in the music video), a seven, "not hot, but warm, like an oven," she described to *Rolling Stone*. "And it smells like cookies." "xanny" is velvety, "like if you could feel smoke." Finneas, who also has synesthesia, is an orange triangle to his sister, yet his name is green. The siblings inherited the neurological phenomenon, which affects as much as 4 percent of the population, from their father, and Billie has joked the three will sometimes have "stupid" disagreements over what color or shape something should be.

"I think the ukulele brings a different feeling to every song. It inspires a different kind of writing."

TOURETTE SYNDROME

When Billie was eleven, she was diagnosed with Tourette syndrome, a disorder that involves uncontrollable repetitive movements or unwanted sounds, known as "tics." For some people, that can range from blinking their eyes to blurting out vulgar words. For Billie, Tourette's manifests as wiggling her ears, raising her eyebrows, or clicking her jaw. Family and friends have always known, but she initially didn't talk about it publicly because "I didn't want that to define who I was," Billie admitted on *The Ellen Show* in 2019. But when a viral clip of her "ticking" was misinterpreted as the famous singer making funny faces, she wanted to set the record straight about Tourette syndrome, which affects an estimated 1.4 million people in the US, according to the Centers for Disease Control and Prevention. "I learned that a lot of my fans have it . . . there was a connection there," and she was happy to use her platform to destigmatize Tourette's for them.

Over the years, Billie has found ways to suppress her tics, especially onstage and in interviews. But occasionally they do come out, like during her 2022 sit-down with David Letterman for his Netflix series, *My Next Guest Needs No Introduction*. In the middle of a question, Billie turned her head and made an exaggerated face. "What's going on? A fly?" asked Letterman looking around, unaware of her Tourette's until she explained. "It's not like I like it, but I feel like it's . . . part of me. I have made friends with it. And so now, I'm pretty confident in it."

UKULELE

At the age of six, Billie learned how to play her first instrument: the ukulele, a small guitar with four strings. After mastering "I Will" by the Beatles, the little girl began making up her own ditties with the few chords she knew (C, G, and F). "I think the ukulele brings a different feeling to every song. It inspires a different kind of writing," Billie said in 2020 when she released her very own ukulele with Fender, a limited-edition matte black four-string adorned with her signature Blohsh symbol that retailed for $299. She hoped people would be inspired like she was to start playing the instrument and write songs of their own. "Basically, the rules of ukulele, like, if you know three chords you know every song ever. Like any song, it's so simple."

VEGAN

Born and raised a vegetarian, at the age of twelve, Billie made the switch to vegan—that means in addition to no meat or fish, she also doesn't eat any animal products like dairy and eggs. Her mother, Maggie, was actually the first person in the family to adopt the diet for health reasons, followed by her father, Patrick, and brother, Finneas. Billie was the lone holdout for years, she told *Los Angeles* magazine in 2023. "My God, did I love cheese and milk. I was very, very against going vegan . . . I guess I just learned about the dairy industry and how much [it] and the meat industry [were] affecting the climate crisis. And affecting people." For Billie—who has never even tasted meat—veganism is not a diet. "It's a way of seeing the world."

In the summer of 2024, she and Finneas revealed plans to open a vegan Italian restaurant, Argento, in the Silver Lake neighborhood of Los Angeles with entrepreneur Nic Adler, son of music producer Lou Adler. "I want plant-based food to be more accessible," Billie explained to *Los Angeles Magazine*. "Vegan is for everyone. You don't have to be vegan to eat vegan. The world is so much better than it was. Ten years ago there was nothing vegan anywhere, and now it's so much more universal." To make it even easier, she created a list of some of her favorite vegan spots across the country, including Monty's Good Burger (Los Angeles), Spicy Moon (New York City), Vedge (Philadelphia), and Cafe Sunflower (Atlanta).

WHERE ARE THE AVOCADOS?

OG Eyelashes might know that Billie's first Instagram handle was @WhereAreTheAvocados. The random (yet totally valid) question originated sometime around 2013, when the youngster was home alone making a grilled cheese sandwich. She wanted to add some slices of avocado but couldn't find them anywhere in the kitchen. "Where are the avocados?" she wondered aloud, searching high and low for the green

> "Vegan is for everyone. You don't have to be vegan to eat vegan. The world is so much better than it was. Ten years ago there was nothing vegan anywhere, and now it's so much more universal."

fruit (yes, technically it's not a vegetable). She never found them, but days later when the twelve-year-old joined Instagram, her imperfect grilled cheese inspired her username. "I was like, 'What was that thing I said? Where are the avocados? That'd be funny as hell,'" Billie recalled to Buzzfeed.

Fans got in on the joke, creating accounts like @HereAreTheAvocados and @ThereAreTheAvocados. After several years as @WhereAreTheAvocados, the singer found her new identity on Instagram, claiming the handle @BillieEilish in 2019.

XXXTENTACION

One of Billie's earliest friends in the industry, the controversial rapper XXXTentacion, was considered a bad influence, but she insisted he got her

through some of her darkest periods. XXXTentacion (real name: Jahseh "Jah" Onfroy) built a cult following in 2017 for his blend of emo-rap and lyrics that delved into depression and alienation. The two bonded over their shared troubles, and even though XXXTentacion had a long rap sheet of charges for drugs and domestic violence, "that was *my* person," she revealed to YouTube channel *Montreality* in 2018, two months after the twenty-year-old rapper was shot and killed in Florida. "He was like a beam of light. That was like the most selfless kid I've ever met in my life, hands down. He'd text me like every day if I was okay. He'd call me and be like, 'Hey, I'm just checking in if you're good.' Who does that?"

Billie was so affected by XXXTentacion's life and death, she wrote the song "6.18.18" about the day he was murdered. Originally meant to appear on *WHEN WE ALL FALL ASLEEP, WHERE DO WE GO?*, it was eventually scrapped. But she did perform it once, telling the crowd that XXXTentacion was someone who "made me feel okay when nothing else did."

YOUNGEST EVER TO . . .

Considering that Billie got her start in the music business at the ripe old age of thirteen, it's no surprise that she's the youngest to set countless records for her achievements. One of her first was in 2019 when her EP *dont smile at me* reached one billion streams on Spotify, making her the youngest artist to ever hit the milestone. With her debut full-length album, *WHEN WE ALL FALL ASLEEP, WHERE DO WE GO?*, she became the youngest female ever to have a number-one album in the UK and the youngest artist in the world since Lorde to have a number-one single with "bad guy."

At seventeen, Billie was the youngest artist in history to be nominated in the Grammy Awards' Big Four general categories—Album of the Year,

> "I'm so so proud of her and in constant awe of her talent and hard work."

Record of the Year, Song of the Year, and Best New Artist—all of which she won in 2020, making her only the second person ever to sweep in a single night (the first was Christopher Cross in 1981, two decades before she was born). That same year, eighteen-year-old Billie took the crown as the youngest headlining act at both the Coachella (US) and Glastonbury (UK) music festivals. Most recently, at the age of twenty-two, Billie earned her second Academy Award for Best Original Song (*Barbie*'s "What Was I Made For?") and became the youngest person to win two Oscars in any category.

ZOE DONAHOE

Billie's BFF is an OG! She's known Zoe since they met as toddlers at a homeschool park day in Highland Park. And when the singer found fame at the age of fifteen, Zoe was the only friend who stayed by Billie's side and has been there ever since. "I'm like her therapy dog, her emotional-support human," Zoe joked to *Rolling Stone* in 2019 when she joined Billie on the When We All Fall Asleep World Tour. Fans got to see their dynamic in the documentary *The World's A Little Blurry*, especially as Billie grieved the end of her relationship with boyfriend Q. Later, during a bout of depression, it was Zoe who helped the superstar overcome her fear of being in public by getting her out of the house and having fun, like when the two attended a My Chemical Romance concert (and sang along to every song) in 2022.

Zoe is much more than just Billie's BFF. A talented photographer, she's shot album covers for several emerging artists and portraits of established acts like Camila Cabello. And, of course, she's documented plenty of behind-the-scenes moments of her best friend, such as at awards shows and birthday celebrations. "I'm so so proud of her and in constant awe of her talent and hard work," Zoe captioned a carousel on Instagram from the 2024 Academy Awards, when Billie won her second Oscar. "I LOVE THIS GIRL SO MUCH THERE ARENT [sic] EVEN WORDS I JUST AM FULL OF LOVE FOR YOU BILLIE."

PART FOUR

What She Was Made For

REINVENTED POP STAR

What you see is only half of what you get with Billie Eilish. She's a complex pop star who has the appearance of a punk and the voice of an angel. She's not your mother's Britney Spears or your grandmother's Madonna; she's Gen Z's pop princess—an outright subversion of every stereotype. This icon doesn't show skin; she covers up in baggy clothing. This girl doesn't just want to have fun; she wants to make an impact. She won't stand by her man; she exposes the "bad guy." Duh.

Billie introduced herself as a deconstructed pop star on her first full studio album, 2019's *WHEN WE ALL FALL ASLEEP, WHERE DO WE GO?*, singing about bad dreams and the monsters under her bed, as well as real-life nightmares like drug addiction, death, mental health, and even climate change. As the teen matured so did her songwriting, although the central themes haven't changed. The COVID-19 pandemic forced her to self-reflect on the sarcastic *Happier Than Ever* (2021). She got existential for the *Barbie* soundtrack, beautifully capturing loneliness with the ballad "What Was I Made For?" (2023). Most recently, Billie explored the extremes of her personality on 2024's *HIT ME HARD AND SOFT*.

It's not just millions of fans around the world who are captivated by Billie. She's also your favorite pop star's favorite pop star. "I love Billie Eilish," Lana Del Rey gushed to *The New York Times* in 2019. "And I feel like I've been waiting for this time in pop music culture." Five years later, the wait for a Lana-Billie collaboration ended when the two sang a mash-up of their breakout hits, Billie's "ocean eyes" and Lana's "Video Games," onstage at Coachella. "That's the voice of our generation, the voice of your generation," Lana told the cheering crowd. "And I'm so fucking grateful she's standing next to me right now." Miley Cyrus has also expressed interest in working with Billie, "one of the coolest artists out there at the moment," as she told the *Mirror* in 2023. "I'm in total awe of her. When I was her age, I didn't know who I was as an artist and was still being heavily influenced by others. But she knows exactly who she is and it is just so impressive." Elton John, whose debut album came out fifty years before Billie's, described the young artist as "a breath of fresh air" to *Music Week* magazine. "There's no one ever like her."

> "I hate smiling. It makes me feel weak and powerless and small. I've always been like that; I don't smile in any pictures."

DON'T TELL HER TO SMILE

From her very first song, "ocean eyes," Billie has conveyed her vulnerability through her music. The title of her debut EP, *dont smile at me*, was literal, not just teenage moodiness. "I hate smiling. It makes me feel weak and powerless and small," the fifteen-year-old revealed to *Harper's Bazaar* in 2017. "I've always been like that; I don't smile in any pictures. If you look at my Instagram, I have a resting bitch face and I guess I just look sad all the time." Sometimes, her expression was genuine. As a child, Billie endured separation anxiety so severe she slept in her parents' bed until she was eleven. Two years later, when injury forced her to quit her beloved dance classes, "that's when the depression started," she confessed to *Rolling Stone* in 2019. "It sent me down a hole . . . we don't have to go into it. But the gist of it was, I felt like I deserved to be in pain."

> *"Songs about being depressed or suicidal or completely just against yourself—some adults think that's bad, but I feel that seeing that someone else feels just as horrible as you do is a comfort."*

Fame at the age of fourteen was not the cure. Despite success with "ocean eyes" becoming a viral sensation, "all I can think of is how miserable I was," Billie told the magazine. "How completely distraught and confused. Thirteen to sixteen was pretty rough." She channeled all those emotions into her 2019 studio album, *WHEN WE ALL FALL ASLEEP, WHERE DO WE GO?*—which some radio stations initially deemed "too sad" to play. Concern that people wouldn't relate "was funny to me because everybody has felt sad in their life," Billie said on *CBS Sunday Morning*. For young people especially, her music resonated. "Kids use my songs as a hug," she explained to *Rolling Stone*. "Songs about being depressed or suicidal or completely just against yourself—some adults think that's bad, but I feel that seeing that someone *else* feels just as horrible as you do is a comfort."

The teen also encouraged people to speak up if they knew someone struggling with mental health. "It doesn't make you weak to ask for a friend to go to a therapist," she said in a 2019 video PSA for the Seize the Awkward campaign. "You know, starting that conversation, you don't have to make it super serious right away, you know, you say, 'How are you feeling? Like, are you okay?'"

It proved hard to take her own advice. Billie remained stuck on an emotional roller coaster throughout her meteoric rise to fame. Ironically, one particularly low point came after *Happier Than Ever*. It was during that "dark episode," when she was questioning everything, that she wrote "What Was I Made For?" for *Barbie*. "I think we all feel like that occasionally," she acknowledged at the 2024 Palm Springs International Film Awards. Personally speaking, Billie admitted there were times "I have really not wanted to be here. I have spent a lot of time feeling that way. But I just want to say to anyone who feels that way: Be patient with yourself."

THEREFORE I AM

Billie is nothing if not candid! In interviews, no topic is truly off-limits—and there's a pretty good chance her answer will be either profound or silly, but always authentic, usually TMI, and most likely punctuated with "dude." She keeps it real, whether she's on the cover of *Rolling Stone* (talking about sex, "literally my favorite topic") or on the red carpet at the Grammy Awards (where in 2023 she indulged in a little toilet humor with *Entertainment Tonight*). In the middle of her appearance on the *Conan O'Brien Needs a Friend* podcast, she earnestly asked, "How loud can you shout? I would like it if you stood in the corner and just shouted as loud as you could." And so Conan did. "That was one of the weirdest moments

of my life," remarked Finneas who has seen it all with his little sister and collaborator.

Take it or leave it, Billie's brutal honesty resonates with millions of people around the world. Ever since she first put out songs on SoundCloud as a teenager, her words have always been embraced by young fans who face the same issues that she does: depression, anxiety, dark thoughts, and self-harm. "People are like, 'You're a role model. People are looking up to you, Billie, how could you possibly say something like that?' You know why they're looking up to me? Because I say shit like that," she told Rob Markman on *For the Record*. "I say what the fuck I want to say because if I don't say it, what's the point?" People's opinions matter so little to Billie, she wrote a song about it: *Happier Than Ever*'s "Therefore I Am," is a title she borrowed from the seventeenth-century phrase "I think therefore I am," which means one is knowledgeable even when they're doubted.

It's not just young fans who feel seen and heard listening to Billie's music. Selena Gomez revealed she "sobbed" when she first heard "everything i wanted," written when Billie was at the height of fame, yet "in a really bad place mentally." Finneas was initially very uncomfortable with the song's subject matter, but Billie's instincts were right: "everything i wanted" hit the Top 10 in two dozen countries—and won Record of the Year at the 2021 Grammys.

MALE FANTASY, FEMALE REALITY

If Billie's music doesn't grab your attention, her style certainly will. Compared to millennial pop stars like Taylor Swift, Beyoncé, and Adele, Gen Z's reigning queen shuns anything even remotely plain or formfitting. "I am not comfortable when I'm wearing just some jeans and a shirt," fifteen-year-old Billie explained in one of her earliest major interviews, with *Harper's Bazaar* in 2017. "I just feel wrong and I feel like very not me and out of my place and just weird."

Billie's unconventional style—oversized clothing, often bordering comical proportions—sparked endless speculation about her body. It was a double standard she could not stand, and any time she was asked about the gender-neutral way she dressed, she gave the questioner an earful. "If I was a guy and I was wearing these baggy clothes, nobody would bat an eye," she told *NME* in 2019. "There's people out there saying, 'Dress like a girl for once! Wear tight clothes you'd be much prettier and your career would be so much better!' No, it wouldn't. It literally would not."

She seemingly had a change of heart in 2021, when she debuted a blonde, glamorous makeover to coincide with her second album, *Happier Than Ever*. But the criticism was just as loud as the compliments. Labeled a sellout, Billie lost one hundred thousand followers on Instagram. "It's very dehumanizing," she admitted to *Elle*. "I had no goal of 'This is going to make everybody think differently of me'. I've had different colored hair and vibes for everything I've ever done. The other day, I posted a video from when I had green hair, and I saw people go, 'I miss this Billie, the green-haired Billie.' I'm still the same person. I'm not just different Barbies with different heads."

Two years later, she played off that idea in her music video for "What Was I Made For?" from the *Barbie* soundtrack. Styled like the original 1959 doll with a sleek blonde ponytail and curled bangs, Billie opens a small clothing trunk and pulls out Barbie-size versions of her most iconic looks *before* her 2021 makeover—the yellow overalls from the "bellyache" video, the black-and-green Gucci suit she wore to the Grammys, and the

> "There's people out there saying, 'Dress like a girl for once! Wear tight clothes you'd be much prettier and your career would be so much better!' No, it wouldn't. It literally would not."

white tweed Chanel set from the Academy Awards—when a storm comes through and threatens to destroy everything she's created. Billie directed the video and explained its concept to *Allure*: "I wanted the world to change and things to change around me, and the world is falling apart as I'm trying to keep these old versions of myself safe."

LOVE IS LOVE

Billie's always been her authentic self, but until 2023 there was one aspect of her personal life she didn't publicize, at least overtly. "I was never planning on talking about my sexuality ever, in a million years," she told *Rolling Stone*. But she had been inadvertently outed on the red carpet of *Variety*'s Hitmakers Brunch when asked about a passing comment she made

> "Nobody should be pressured into being one thing or the other, and I think that there's a lot of wanting labels all over the place."

that she was physically attracted to women. "Did you mean to come out in that story?" laughed a reporter for the magazine. "No I didn't," Billie replied. "But I kind of thought, 'Wasn't it obvious?' . . . I've been doing this for a long time, and I just didn't talk about it. Whoops." After the event, however, she expressed frustration with being ambushed by such a personal question. "Thanks *Variety* for my award and for also outing me on a red carpet at 11 a.m. instead of talking about anything else that matters," the singer wrote on Instagram. "I like boys and girls leave me alone about it please literally who cares."

Everyone did, it seemed. Billie's bisexuality made headlines and was overwhelmingly well-received. "Billie Eilish, Welcome to the Queer-Pop-Girlie Canon," proclaimed *Vogue*. She was happy to be a part of the musical movement (alongside the likes of Janelle Monae, Kehlani, and Reneé Rapp), but wished she could have controlled how the world learned such a personal matter. "Nobody should be pressured into being one thing or the other, and I think that there's a lot of wanting labels all over the place," she told *Rolling Stone*. "I know everybody's been thinking this about me for years and years, but I'm only figuring out myself now." The "Brunch" conversation led to "LUNCH," as she metaphorically explored her appetite for the same sex in the lead single off her 2024 album, *HIT ME HARD AND SOFT*.

    Looking back, Billie had dropped some not-so-subtle hints. "I love girls," she captioned a photo from the "Lost Cause" music video, which centers around a sexually suggestive slumber party. In 2022, during a fan Q&A on Instagram, she was asked about her childhood crush—and for once, she didn't say Justin Bieber. The famous person whom young Billie had a thing for was actually *Buffy the Vampire Slayer* actress Sarah Michelle Gellar. No one was more astounded by the revelation than Gellar, who took a screenshot of Billie's answer and reposted it on her own Instagram feed. "I'm dead. That's all," she captioned the photo. "I'm not a child anymore, but I totally have a crush on @billieeilish." The prestige also earned the actress cool points with her teenage son and daughter. However, she did have one concern about being Billie's *childhood* crush: "So I'm not anymore? Who replaced me?"

SIBLING SYNERGY

Behind every great Billie Eilish song is a great songwriter: her older brother, Finneas. Ever since their first collaboration, 2015's "ocean eyes," the O'Connell siblings have been the most dynamic duo in music, churning out dozens of hit singles worth $45.5 million in digital sales (according to the Recording Industry Association of America), eighty billion streams, nine Grammy Awards, and two Academy Awards.

Each is uniquely talented, complementing the other's artistic strengths. Finneas is a musical genius who excels at writing and producing music that Billie brings to life with her ethereal vocals. "I've always thought I was a terrible songwriter," Billie confessed in 2019 during a Q&A session at the Grammy Museum. "We're four years apart. He started writing at twelve. Me, too, but four years later. It was annoying how good he was. Because he's always been so good, it makes me feel bad." Finneas, sitting beside Billie onstage, piped up to brag about his sister. "Her pitch is dead-on all the time," he noted, and it was her voice that defined "when the party's over," a standout on her debut album. Until Finneas brought a draft of the track to Billie, "it had a universal quality," he explained. "[But I knew that] she could interpret the song and do it way better than I ever could." Indeed, she turned it into a stark ballad that relies solely on her vocal talent, which Finneas recorded as one hundred tracks that he then layered to create each harmony.

When Billie signed a record deal in 2016 following the viral success of "ocean eyes"—a song that Finneas originally wrote for his band, the Slightlys—the label steered the teenager toward working with veteran songwriters, instead of her brother (who was still a teenager himself). "I hated it so much," Billie recalled to *Rolling Stone* of those early studio sessions. "It was always these fifty-year-old men who'd written these 'big hit songs!' and then they're horrible at it. I'm like, 'You did this a hundred years ago. Ugh.' No one listened to me, because I was fourteen and a girl. And we made 'ocean eyes' without anyone involved—so why are we doing this?" Ultimately, Billie won the battle to bring Finneas back into the fold, and he continues to enjoy his role as his sister's not-so-secret weapon. "We've never billed it as a duo," he pointed out at their Grammy Museum event. "It's so important that it's her vision. I don't have anything to do with the visuals. It's her singing the songs."

Following the success of *WHEN WE ALL FALL ASLEEP, WHERE DO WE GO?*, Finneas moved out of the family home where he and Billie had written and recorded dozens of songs, and admittedly, she feared they'd struggle to recapture the magic they had created inside his tiny bedroom. But she needn't have worried: Finneas built a super studio in the basement of his $2.73 million historic home in Los Feliz, just a short drive from where the siblings grew up in Highland Park. Together in the new (and slightly improved) space, the siblings built upon their early success with Billie's second album, *Happier Than Ever*, which earned seven Grammy nominations. Specifically, Finneas witnessed the singer blossoming as a songwriter. "It's been awesome as a big brother to see her become more confident and feel more ownership and just to be more excited than I've ever seen her about the music that we're making," he told *Rolling Stone* in 2021. "I also just think she has objectively gotten even better. That's my opinion. If she were an Olympic gymnast or something, she would've gotten better. She'd be able to do a higher vault or something."

Not long after completing *Happier Than Ever*, a pipe burst at Finneas's home and completely flooded the studio, yet miraculously spared the hard drives storing Billie's music catalog. They rebuilt the room just as it had been, since "it was effective for us," Finneas explained in a joint Apple Music interview with his sister. However, they utilized the space very differently when they returned to make her third full-length album, 2024's *HIT ME HARD AND SOFT*. Instead of recording her vocals from a nearby couch, Billie sat beside her brother "like pilots in an airplane."

Ultimately, Finneas took a back seat in the studio as his little sister's evolution as an artist became undeniable. And as siblings are wont to do, they occasionally butted heads, especially any time the big brother propped his bare feet up on the sound board in front of Billie. However, during a "period of transition in maybe both of our lives," the mood got tense, Finneas recalled on *Hot Ones Versus*, in between bites of spicy vegan chicken wings. "To give [Billie] credit, I was very much high and mighty about, like, 'You're not being honest or authentic enough.' So I learned a lot from being too egocentric in that process."

As their dynamic shifted, so did Billie's perspective on making music. In the past, she had found it so stressful she sometimes wanted to quit altogether. Now, it was finally enjoyable for her, but not for Finneas. "It was very interesting because I saw myself in that," Billie admitted during their interview with Apple's Zane Lowe. "I was like, 'I have felt that way and you have always been the thing that keeps the ship moving, and now you feel that way. What does that mean for us? And what are we going to do?'"

It was decided that Billie would take on more of the songwriting, something that excited and terrified her in equal measures. "We've been making music for years and I've been shy and not very quick with it, and I've never felt confident as a songwriter," she explained to Lowe. But with their roles now swapped, she was forced to step outside her comfort zone and tap into the abilities Finneas knew she possessed. Any time she got stuck during the creative process, "he would sit there . . . and not say anything or give any ideas. I'd be like, 'I don't even know what I'm supposed to do.' [But] it pushed me to actually do so much. This album was the most I've ever written and contributed."

BEYOND BILLIE

Finneas is so prolific, he has written enough material for two of his own solo albums, *Blood Harmony* (2019) and *Optimist* (2021), as well as songs for some of today's biggest pop stars, including Camila Cabello, Demi Lovato, Halsey, and Tove Lo. In 2020, he scored a number-one hit with Selena Gomez, who hired Billie's brother to work his magic on "Lose You to Love Me." Although Finneas downplayed his involvement, saying he just added some string plucks and synths, Selena praised him for putting "the final touch" on the ballad. "It just really made a difference from the second chorus into what he did in the bridge," she told Sirius XM. Coincidentally, that same year Finneas worked with the person who had caused Selena's heartbreak, Justin Bieber, on the Grammy-nominated "Lonely." In between recording with Billie, he also contributed two songs to Kid Cudi's *Man on the Moon III: The Chosen* and wrote "I Still Say Goodnight" with TikTok viral sensation Tate McRae. But his sister doesn't need to worry about losing her secret weapon. "Billie takes precedence over all," he insisted to Howard Stern. "Billie's first, always."

HARD, YET SOFT

Billie's signature style is streetwear: oversized silhouettes in bright neon fabric, often monogrammed or graffitied, and always accessorized with sunglasses, sneakers, and hats. She dresses for comfort, but primarily to feel comfortable in the public eye (and her own skin). "I never want the world to know everything about me. I mean, that's why I wear big, baggy clothes," Billie explained in a 2019 campaign ad for Calvin Klein. "Nobody can have an opinion because they haven't seen what's underneath, you know? Nobody can be like, 'Oh, she's slim-thick, she's not slim-thick, she's got a flat ass, she's got a fat ass.' No one can say any of that, because they don't know."

She did give fans a quick glimpse in 2021, when she slipped into a corset for the May cover of British *Vogue*. The pictorial transformed the tomboy into a classic pin-up model with a custom wardrobe of waist-cinching pieces by Gucci, Alexander McQueen, Thierry Mugler, and Burberry. Anticipating backlash for the uncharacteristically sexy makeover, Billie insisted it only emphasized her belief in body positivity. "My thing is that I can do whatever I want," she told the magazine. "It's all about what makes you feel good . . . Showing your body and showing your skin—or not—should not take any respect away from you."

Although the super-glam version of Billie didn't last beyond the pages of *Vogue*, she has continued to embrace her femininity on the red carpet. These are five unforgettable looks that tapped into her style's softer side.

MARILYN MOMENT

Billie's interpretation of the Met Gala's 2021 theme, "In America: A Lexicon of Fashion," channeled iconic sex symbol Marilyn Monroe. The newly blonde singer stunned in a custom Oscar de la Renta peach tulle, off-the-shoulder gown inspired by a similar black dress Marilyn wore to the 1951 Academy Awards (which the up-and-coming actress borrowed from the 20th Century Fox wardrobe department). Billie also proved diamonds are a girl's best friend in thirty pieces of Cartier jewelry, including twenty-five rings—the most ever worn on a red carpet, according to *Vogue*.

The singer's collaboration with de la Renta was bigger than the fashion moment they created: She convinced the design house to permanently cease using fur in all its clothing lines. "I am so beyond thrilled that [they] heard me on this issue and have made a change that not only makes an impact for the greater good for animals but also for our planet and

> "My thing is that I can do whatever I want. It's all about what makes you feel good... Showing your body and showing your skin—or not—should not take any respect away from you."

environment too," the vegan activist told the magazine. "I'm honored to have been a catalyst and to have been heard on this matter. I urge all designers to do the same."

HOSTESS CUPCAKE

It's not every day we see Billie in a dress, let alone one that looks like a frilly festive cupcake. For her first time as both host and musical guest on *Saturday Night Live* in December 2021, the twenty-year-old got in the holiday spirit, opening the show decked out in a poofy white dress made of lace and tulle and adorned with embroidered red bows, designed by Simone Rocha. "You may know me from my music, you may know me for my hair or my clothes, that's why I decided to dress like Mrs. Claus going to the club," Billie joked in her monologue. "But actually, no. I'm only wearing this because after the show I gotta go get married in an animé."

Jokes aside, the whimsical fashion moment went viral in real time, as the episode aired live from New York. The playful dress was a standout of Rocha's Spring 2022 ready-to-wear collection, which focused on themes of motherhood and birth featuring several pieces inspired by christening gowns.

DRAMATIC ENTRANCE

Billie commanded attention when she arrived at the 2023 *Vanity Fair* Oscar after-party in a billowy black gown so voluminous it could barely fit in the frame of photos when splayed out on the red carpet. Designed by Rick Owens, who also dressed the singer at the 2022 Grammy Awards, the dramatic look was actually sheer at the bodice (Billie wore a corset underneath) with tiers of tulle that built out the bulk. The top half was simpler, with a chevron pattern cascading down the shoulders and a deep V-neckline, which she accessorized with Chrome Hearts jewelry.

The showstopper looked cool in photos, but it wasn't exactly practical—Billie nearly tripped on the red carpet when one of her towering platform heels got caught in the fabric as she walked over to her then-boyfriend Jesse Rutherford. On social media, the look was polarizing, as fans were split over whether Billie was "giving mother" or, as one put it, "giving loofah."

GOTH CHICK

Billie ventured to the dark side in 2023 for her third appearance at the Met Gala: a head-to-toe black sheer ensemble, done in lace, tulle, tinsel cotton, and crystal embellishments. Her glam was just as goth, with kohl-rimmed eyes, sheer black gloves up to her elbows, and a black ribbon braided into her raven-colored hair, lengthened by extensions down to her waist. Custom-designed by "my girl" Simone Rocha, the high-necked dress was Billie's vision brought to life. "I wanted to do layers, lots of textures, lots of fabrics, materials. I wanted things hanging," she told *Vogue*'s Emma Chamberlain on the red carpet.

With that directive, Rocha pulled together a one-of-a-kind look befitting the pop star. "I was inspired by Billie herself, her talent, her world, and her powerful femininity," the Irish designer said in a statement. "I wanted to celebrate her femininity through fragility and strength. Working with fragile tulle and edging it in lace, interpreting embellishment as armor, and creating a look which reflected an emotion, a very layered piece revealing what lies beneath . . ."

TRAIL BLAZER

Billie was all business at the 2024 Academy Awards: the Best Original Song winner accepted her second Oscar statuette in a black blazer, white tuxedo shirt with a high collar, and black-and-white tweed pencil skirt all by Chanel, paired with black Mary Jane heels worn with white socks. "I would say it's like a substitute teacher vibe," she joked to *Extra* on the red carpet before the ceremony. Billie specifically chose the luxury fashion house for good luck—she was wearing a black Chanel gown when she won her first Oscar in 2022 for "No Time to Die."

For her performance of "What Was I Made For?," Billie swapped her black blazer for an oversized coat in black denim ribbon tweed from Thom Browne's Fall 2024 collection. Her dainty accessories were a nod to the song's inspiration, Barbie: a ribbon tie and headband both in pink, the iconic doll's signature color.

YOUNG AND RESTLESS

"Yeah, we're all going to die soon," Billie deadpanned to *Billboard* in a 2024 interview about protecting the environment. "But we can try our best." The pop star has absolutely gone above and beyond in her never-ending quest to make the world a better place, leveraging her global platform to raise awareness about climate change, women's rights, animal rights, body positivity, and food insecurity. Billie integrates solutions into every aspect of her artistry, from sustainable merchandise to concerts partially powered by zero-emissions battery systems.

> *"I'm still not shoving information down people's throats. I'm more like, I'm not going to tell you what to do. I'm just going to tell you why I do this."*

"I've spent all of my effort trying not to be in people's faces about it because people don't respond well to that," Billie admitted to *Vogue*. "It makes the causes that you believe in look bad, because you're, like, annoying the shit out of everybody. I'm still not shoving information down people's throats. I'm more like, I'm not going to tell you what to do. I'm just going to tell you why I do this."

SAVE THE PLANET

Raised in an eco-conscious household, Billie was "green" long before she dyed her hair the color: her family used dish towels instead of recycled paper napkins and their Los Angeles home ran on solar power. As an artist, she's carried on those environmentally friendly habits. On all her tours, plastic straws are banned and single-use plastic eliminated: Fans and crew members drink from reusable water bottles that can be filled at free hydration stations and venues are also asked to serve beverages in their original container (instead of pouring into a plastic cup).

According to Reverb, a nonprofit Billie partnered with to reduce her Happier Than Ever, The World Tour's environmental footprint, 117,000 single-use water bottles were avoided. Additionally, 8.8 million gallons (33 million L) of water were saved by serving plant-based meals to the artists and crew. At each stop, ecovillages provided information on the climate crisis to fans, who donated $116,000, and Billie herself dedicated a portion of ticket sales to support climate justice, carbon reduction, and ocean resilience. In London, ahead of her six sold-out shows at the O2 Arena in June 2022, the singer hosted Overheated, a conference for a hundred music industry professionals to discuss climate action with experts. It was such a success, she organized a second summit the following September that was livestreamed on YouTube for fans around the world.

In 2023, Billie funded and launched Reverb's Music Decarbonization Project, which aims to eliminate all carbon emissions released into the atmosphere by the music industry. She made the first step at that summer's Lollapalooza festival in Chicago by partially powering her set with zero-emissions battery systems charged on a "solar farm," technology that replaces highly polluting diesel generators with clean energy. The work expanded for her 2024–25 Hit Me Hard and Soft: The Tour: Reverb established ecovillages in two locations at each of the eighty-one shows, maximizing outreach to fans they hope will be inspired to "take meaningful action for people and the planet."

WASTE NOT, WANT NOT

Billie is such a stickler for sustainability: "I'm so unable to just throw things away in the trash," she confessed to *Billboard* in 2024. "Like, it's genuinely annoying. I wish I just didn't care and could throw it all in the garbage and that could be the end of it." But that's not how she was raised. In the Baird-O'Connell home, "you got the stink eye if you came in with a plastic bag or if you wasted anything," added her mother Maggie. Those principles have guided how Billie produces merchandise for her fans' consumption. All clothing is made from a variety of 100 percent recycled cotton, organic cotton, or recycled polyester. Posters are also 100 percent recycled paper. It's a little more complicated for vinyl records: All are made using recyclable or recycled compounds, as is the packaging—even the ink is raw plant-based and water-based dispersion varnish. And at Billie's merch booths, her website makes it clear: "No plastic bags are offered on tour."

In an era of fast fashion, Billie is mindful to not contribute to the detriment of the planet. She purposely limits her merch drops and vinyl releases—and when she sees other artists not doing their part, she feels she must say something. "It's some of the biggest artists in the world making fucking forty different vinyl packages that have a different unique thing just to get you to keep buying more," Billie told *Billboard* in March 2024. It was widely speculated she was referencing Taylor Swift, who had just announced six vinyl versions of *The Tortured Poets Department*. "It's so wasteful, and it's irritating to me that we're still at a point where you care that much about your numbers and you care that much about making money—and it's all your favorite artists doing that shit."

HOMETOWN HERO

As a Los Angeles native, Billie was personally touched by the January 2025 fires that devastated the city, destroying thousands of homes in Altadena and Pasadena, two neighborhoods located just miles from where she grew up in Highland Park. In an effort to provide relief to victims, the superstar helped raise $100 million as part of FireAid, a six-hour benefit concert featuring Lady Gaga, Katy Perry, Pink, Stevie Nicks, and Jelly Roll that was held simultaneously at two local venues. Billie first took the stage at Kia Forum to join Green Day for the band's song "Last Night on Earth," and then headed to Intuit Dome a few blocks away just in time to perform an acoustic set with Finneas. "To everyone who's going through this, I love you and I got you," Billie told the crowd. "I will not forget about you, and we will keep doing this for you." One special fan felt the singer's kindness firsthand: When she learned a fifteen-year-old girl had lost her Hit Me Hard and Soft Tour T-shirt in the fire, Billie sent her the entire merchandise collection plus an autographed copy of the album on vinyl.

WE CAN DO IT

"Being a woman is just such a war, forever," Billie mused to *Variety* in 2023, when the magazine honored her at its Power of Women event. In her speech, the twenty-one-year-old was uncharacteristically emotional, fighting back tears as she confessed, "I've spent a lot of my life not feeling like I fit in to being a woman . . . And I have to say, with full transparency, I feel very grateful to be a woman right now." The year before, she stood onstage at the Glastonbury Festival, as 1.2 million people watched live on BBC, and voiced her anger over the Supreme Court's decision to end the constitutional right to abortion. "Today is a really, really dark day for women in the US," Billie told the crowd, before performing "Your Power," about people who abuse authority.

The overturning of Roe v. Wade—which Billie described as "a curtain of doom"—also inspired a new song: "TV," which trivializes the more popular news story at the time—the defamation suit Johnny Depp brought against his ex-wife Amber Heard. "Women are losing rights for their bodies, so why are we talking about celebrities' divorce trials?" Billie remarked to *NME*. "Who gives a shit? Let them figure it out on their own. The internet bothers the shit out of me sometimes." Two years later, as the US Senate continued to battle over women's reproductive rights, Billie announced her endorsement of the 2024 presidential candidate who pledged to restore a woman's right to choose, Vice President Kamala Harris. "Vote like your life depends on it," the singer told her 119 million Instagram followers, "because it does."

NOT HER RESPONSIBILITY

Since her teens, Billie has attempted to silence any speculation about her body by hiding it under baggy clothes. "I wasn't trying to have

> "I've spent a lot of my life not feeling like I fit in to being a woman . . . And I have to say, with full transparency, I feel very grateful to be a woman right now."

people *not* sexualize me," she explained to *Variety*. "But I didn't want people to have access to my body, even visually . . . I've had big boobs since I was nine years old, and that's just the way I am. That's how I look. You wear something that's at all revealing, and everyone's like, 'Oh, but you didn't want people to sexualize you?'. . . Nobody ever says a thing about men's bodies. If you're muscular, cool. If you're not, cool. If you're rail thin, cool. If you have a dad bod, cool. If you're pudgy, love it! Everybody's happy with it. You know why? Because girls are nice."

Billie was so fired up about the double standard, she directed a short film on the issue, *Not My Responsibility*, which she premiered in 2020 on her Where Do We Go? World Tour as an interlude. In the nearly four-minute clip, the singer slowly takes off layers of clothing in a dimly lit

> "We make assumptions about people based on their size. We decide who they are. We decide what they're worth. Is my value based only on your perception? Or is your opinion of me not my responsibility?"

room, as she shares her frustrations in a voiceover. "We make assumptions about people based on their size. We decide who they are. We decide what they're worth," Billie muses, as she ultimately sinks into black water once she takes off her shirt. "Is my value based only on your perception? Or is your opinion of me not my responsibility?" The short film was also uploaded to her YouTube account, where it has since racked up over forty million views.

To her dismay, it didn't silence body-shamers. Only months later, Billie was photographed by paparazzi walking into her brother's house dressed in a tank top and knee-length shorts. "People were like, 'Damn, Billie got fat,' and I'm like, 'Nope, this is how I look, you've just never seen it before,'" she told *Vanity Fair*. But she refused to let trolls make her feel bad. "I love having kids relate to me and tell me that I make them feel comfortable in their bodies. If I can do anything, I want to do that."

POWERED BY PLANTS

The animal lover went vegan at the age of twelve, and as she learned more about the plant-based lifestyle, she discovered the impact of the meat industry on climate change. One fact that especially shocked her is that it takes approximately 460 gallons (1,471 L) of water to produce *one* quarter-pound hamburger (according to the US Geological Survey). At Billie's concerts, one of the many informational booths set up in the ecovillage encourages fans to pledge to eat one fully plant-based meal a day. "I really don't like shoving information down people's throats. And nobody wants to be told what to do," she acknowledged to *Variety*. "But I just want to make sure everyone knows the deal, and then make your decision. What I really don't like is just being ignorant about it and being comfortable in that."

While she's self-aware about coming off too preachy, Billie is thoughtful of how her message can make the greatest impact. She performed at the 2023 Global Citizen Festival in Paris as part of the organization's Power Our Planet campaign, and backstage with millions around the world watching the livestream, she advocated for veganism. "For me, the most important thing you can do is changing what's on your plate and what you're eating—to try and end animal agriculture," she told viewers. "Eating a more plant-based diet is really really important. I mean, you have no idea how absolutely horrendous it is for the environment."

Billie puts her money where her mouth is, only partnering with brands that honor her animal-friendly ethics. In 2023, she convinced Gucci to launch a non-leather handbag line. Her most significant accomplishment, she believes, is convincing Oscar de la Renta to stop using fur in its luxury fashion line in 2021. "That was really important to me," she told *Billboard*. "It's tough as a person who loves fashion. I've tried to be a big advocate of no animal products in clothing and it's hard. People really like classic things. I get it, I'm one of them. But what's more important: things being original or our kids being able to live on the planet and them having kids?"

LIKE MOTHER, LIKE DAUGHTER

The apple doesn't fall far from the tree: Billie inherited her activist spirit from her mother, Maggie. The dynamic duo joined forces to establish Support + Feed, a nonprofit that addresses climate change and food equity while moving society to a more plant-based system. It all began with Maggie in 2020, when the pandemic necessitated a crisis-relief operation to distribute vegan food to those in need. Within four years, Support + Feed has reached forty-one cities and delivered nearly six hundred thousand meals and pantry items. That success is due in large part to Billie's influence and platform: She put the nonprofit front and center in the ecovillage at her back-to-back sold-out world tours. In 2023, Maggie honored her daughter at the first annual Support + Feed fundraiser; however, Billie used her acceptance speech to shine the spotlight on her mother who "I'm so in awe of," she gushed to attendees. "And I every day aspire to be more like you. This is such an incredible thing that you have done . . . It is such an amazing thing. And I'm so impressed by you. And I'm so proud of you."

BIRDS OF A FEATHER

The singer's flock of friends is as diverse as her musical tastes, with famous pals spanning the worlds of pop, rock, and rap, as well as several hailing from Hollywood. Becoming an overnight success at fourteen changed everything for Billie, particularly her childhood friendships. "I suddenly was famous, and I couldn't relate to anybody and it was really hard," she confessed on Lily Allen's podcast, *Miss Me?* in June 2024. Billie instead bonded with those on her team, most of whom were decades older, until one employee quit out of the blue and never spoke to her again.

"I kind of had this realization, like, 'Oh, I might actually be alone for real,'" she recounted to Allen and her cohost, Miquita Oliver. "Then I worked really hard on friendship and making friends and making new friends and rekindling old friendships. About exactly a year ago, I reconnected with a bunch of old friends, and now I have so many friends; I have a crew now! I could literally cry about it. It's been the greatest thing that's ever happened to me . . . I couldn't go on without friends. My friendships are, like, the best part of my life."

JUSTIN BIEBER

Billie went from fan to friend the moment she bumped into the "Baby" singer while dancing to NSYNC at the 2019 Coachella Music Festival. Three months later, they collaborated on a remix of "bad guy," and ever since, the Biebs, who also rose to fame as a preteen, has vowed to be a good guy to Billie. "I definitely feel protective of her," he tearfully told Apple Music's Zane Lowe in an emotional 2020 interview. "I don't want her to go through anything I went through. I don't wish that upon anybody. If she ever needs me, I'm just a call away." And he's kept his word. Billie has gushed about how grateful she is for Bieber's unconditional support. "He really makes me feel so loved and seen," she revealed on the podcast *Conan O'Brien Needs a Friend*, "and he's always reaching out to me in the sweetest ways, in the most, like, just comforting ways of just like, 'You're not alone in this, I was there.'"

LANA DEL REY

Two of the coolest women in music have one of the most enviable friendships, built upon their mutual admiration as both artists and

> "About exactly a year ago, I reconnected with a bunch of old friends, and now I have so many friends; I have a crew now! I could literally cry about it. It's been the greatest thing that's ever happened to me"

humans. Fans got a peek into their dynamic in a phone call published in the February 2023 issue of *Interview*. Lana revealed that somehow Billie got her number and reached out one day just as she had pulled her car over to make an important decision. "You literally texted me saying something like, 'I love you, and without you, I wouldn't have been able to do certain things,'" she reminded Billie. "I was like, 'I made the right decision because Billie texted me.'" The twenty-one-year-old was overwhelmed with emotion. "I am always going to ride and die for you," she told Lana. The two reunited for *Interview* again in 2024, and what was supposed to be a phone call to discuss *HIT ME HARD AND SOFT* turned into a video chat so the

> *"I am always going to ride and die for you."*

giggly pair could genuinely connect. "You know how much I love you and how much talking to you means to me," Billie gushed to Lana.

HARRY STYLES

More colleagues than close friends, Billie and the former One Direction heartthrob share a unique kinship that was electric at the 2021 Grammy Awards, as they sparked more interest than the show itself on social media. The two superstars—both decked out in custom Gucci—acted like each other's biggest fans: Billie watched adoringly as Harry performed "Watermelon Sugar." After Styles beat her for the Best Pop Solo

Performance award, he walked offstage and straight to Billie for a hug. The following year, they co-headlined Coachella and Billie was one of the one hundred thousand in attendance to see Harry's set, and she very sternly shushed anyone who didn't give him their undivided attention. "Literally, these motherfuckers were talking so loud, and I turned around and I was like, 'Shut the fuck up and listen to this fucking song,'" she laughed recalling the moment to Apple Music's Zane Lowe. "And everybody was like, 'Damn! Jesus Christ.'"

OLIVIA RODRIGO

Just like veteran artists kept an eye on Billie as she was coming up in the industry, she has done the same for Rodrigo, who at seventeen became the youngest to top the *Billboard* Hot 100 chart with "Driver's License." Billie saw herself in the former Disney Channel star and it inspired her to write 2021's "GOLDWING," about an ingénue at risk of exploitation. But she didn't reveal her muse—not even to Rodrigo—until 2023, when the two had become close friends. "I felt so nervous. I was worried about her," Billie confessed to the *Los Angeles Times*. "I just felt very protective over her." Rodrigo, who is only fourteen months younger, appreciated the support from her pal. "Billie is such a kind, wonderful girl," she also told the *LA Times*, "and I feel very lucky that it's not about competition—that we're just looking out for each other."

DAKOTA JOHNSON

Perhaps one of the stranger pairings, the *Fifty Shades of Grey* actress and Billie are so tight, the actor can be honest with the singer when she's

making a mistake (or so she thinks). In 2024, Billie pranked Johnson for *Elle*'s "Phoning It In" video series, seeking advice on a movie role she had been offered—albeit, playing a baby in a diaper. Just as Billie predicted, Johnson generously considered her friend's quandary. "Is it a good script?" she asked. "Is it meant to be funny or serious?" Dakota's interest turned to skepticism, however, when Billie asked if she knew a dialect coach. "That was the question?" she laughed. "I thought it was like, 'Should I do this job?'" Billie eventually admitted it was all a joke, but Dakota got the last laugh. "Can you imagine if my next thing to say was like, 'Don't you have enough money already?'"

TYLER, THE CREATOR

Among Billie's many goals in the music industry was meeting her idol, Tyler, The Creator. During the promotion of 2017's *dont smile at me*, she name-checked the Odd Future rapper everywhere from MTV's *TRL* to *Vanity Fair* hoping to get his attention—and it worked. In 2018, she was happy to report "I met him and it was great." It turned out Tyler was just as big of a fan. "I like her. I just want her to keep doing her goddamn thing," he told Zane Lowe. The two artists released albums within weeks of each other in 2019, and Tyler's *Igor* debuted at No. 1, "and then this seventeen-year-old girl dressed like a quarterback decided to change that," he joked at the American Music Awards, where he introduced Billie's performance of "all the good girls go to hell." Tyler was one of the unsuspecting friends Billie pranked for *Elle*, and he proved he'd be there through thick and thin, and otherwise. Billie told him she had soiled her pants while on a date and needed to come to his house for a change of clothes. "Um, alright," he replied, although he was more curious with how she ended up in the predicament. Billie admitted it was a joke and apologized, but Tyler was amused, telling her, "Love you, you a thug."

ZOE KRAVITZ

When Billie won her first Academy Award in 2022, the statuette was presented by *The Batman* actress, one of her newer Hollywood friends. In a cute moment caught by cameras after her acceptance speech, Billie put her arm around Kravitz and the two jumped up and down as they exited the stage. Kravitz was there during the tough times too. When the singer repeatedly flaked on plans during an "existential crisis," Kravitz confronted Billie, who was just starstruck and afraid of rejection. "[W]hat if you don't like me?" she recalled to *Rolling Stone*. "I think I probably just told her to shut up and get over it," Kravitz told the magazine. "And we've been really good friends ever since. It's actually the opposite of what she said: The more I get to know her, she gets better and better."

"And we've been really good friends ever since. It's actually the opposite of what she said: The more I get to know her, she gets better and better."

ACKNOWLEDGMENTS

An entire generation older than Billie, I guess I'm considered an Elder Eyelash. And as someone who became a fan a little later than most, I particularly enjoyed retracing her steps to super-stardom through video interviews, especially Apple Music's Zane Lowe and *Vanity Fair*'s "Time Capsule" series, both of which illustrate Billie's evolution as an artist and young woman. Her many sit-downs with *Rolling Stone* and *Vogue* over the years also helped me understand the mind behind the musical genius.

ABOUT THE AUTHOR

Kathleen Perricone is a freelance writer of long-form magazines (bookazines) with published titles about Marilyn Monroe, John F. Kennedy, Anne Frank, Barack Obama, Taylor Swift, Beyoncé, and dozens more. Over the past two decades, Kathleen has also worked as a celebrity news editor in New York City as well as for Yahoo!, Ryan Seacrest Productions, and a reality TV family who shall remain nameless. She lives in Los Angeles.

© 2025 by Quarto Publishing Group USA Inc.
Text © 2025 by Kathleen Perricone

First published in 2025 by Epic Ink, an imprint of The Quarto Group,
142 West 36th Street, 4th Floor, New York, NY 10018, USA
(212) 779-4972 • www.Quarto.com

All rights reserved. No part of this book may be reproduced in any form without written permission of the copyright owners. All images included in this book are original works created by the artist credited on the copyright page, not generated by artificial intelligence, and have been reproduced with the knowledge and prior consent of the artist. The producer, publisher, and printer accept no responsibility for any infringement of copyright or otherwise arising from the contents of this publication. Every effort has been made to ensure that credits accurately comply with information supplied. We apologize for any inaccuracies that may have occurred and will resolve inaccurate or missing information in a subsequent reprinting of the book.

Epic Ink titles are also available at discount for retail, wholesale, promotional, and bulk purchase. For details, contact the Special Sales Manager by email at specialsales@quarto.com or by mail at The Quarto Group, Attn: Special Sales Manager, 100 Cummings Center Suite 265D, Beverly, MA 01915 USA.

10 9 8 7 6 5 4 3 2 1

ISBN: 978-0-7603-9686-5

Digital edition published in 2025
eISBN: 978-0-7603-9687-2

Library of Congress Cataloging-in-Publication Data

Names: Perricone, Kathleen, author.
Title: Billie Eilish is life : a superfan's guide to all things we love about Billie Eilish / Kathleen Perricone.
Description: New York : Epic Ink, 2025. | Series: Modern icons | Summary: "Billie Eilish Is Life is a beautifully illustrated guide that explores and celebrates the performer, her music, and her wide-ranging career"--Provided by publisher.
Identifiers: LCCN 2024056484 | ISBN 9780760396865 (hardcover) | ISBN 9780760396872 (ebook)
Subjects: LCSH: Eilish, Billie, 2001- | Singers--United States--Biography. | LCGFT: Biographies. | Discographies.
Classification: LCC ML420.E354 P47 2025 | DDC 782.42164092 [B]--dc23/eng/20241122
LC record available at https://lccn.loc.gov/2024056484

Group Publisher: Rage Kindelsperger
Creative Director: Laura Drew
Managing Editor: Cara Donaldson
Editors: Katie McGuire and Flannery Wiest
Cover and Interior Design: Beth Middleworth
Book Layout: Danielle Smith-Boldt
Illustrations: Carolina Fuenmayor

Printed in China

This publication has not been prepared, approved, or licensed by the author, producer, or owner of any motion picture, television program, book, game, blog, or other work referred to herein. This is not an official or licensed publication. We recognize further that some words, models' names, and designations mentioned herein are the property of the trademark holder. We use them for identification purposes only.